THE GROWTH OF LONDON

THE GROWTH OF LONDON

by

DEREK MAYNE

GEORGE G. HARRAP & CO. LTD
LONDON TORONTO WELLINGTON SYDNEY

Specially published in this edition 1953

*Composed in Bembo type and printed by Western Printing Services Ltd.
Bristol. Made in Great Britain*

PREFACE

THIS book is no more than an introduction to a vast, complicated, but endlessly fascinating subject. It grew out of researches undertaken in the making of an educational film for Messrs G.-B. Instructional, Ltd, which also was called *The Growth of London*. Most of the illustrations in this book are taken from drawings used in that film.

No one can write a book of this sort without being indebted to a host of others who have written about some aspects of this great subject. A list of those found most useful is given at page 140, in the belief that others also will find them helpful in further reading.

Many maps and plans have been consulted. Ralph Agas drew a picture-plan of London in Elizabethan times (about 1560) which has been reproduced by the London Topographical Society. It is available in the British Museum. A large selection of maps and plans of London from that date onward is to be found in the Crace Collection, in the Map Room of the British Museum, and there are others in the Guildhall Library. The four maps illustrating the distribution of London's population are reproduced by courtesy of the Pictorial Charts Unit.

Special mention must be made of the excellent volume of carefully selected writings about London through the ages entitled *The London Anthology*, by Hugh and Pauline Massingham, published by Phœnix House, Ltd, from which the illustration of Bear-baiting and many of the quotations used in this book have been borrowed.

D.M.

CONTENTS

ILLUSTRATIONS

Plates in Half-tone

Line Drawings in the Text

Chapter One

PREHISTORIC AND ROMAN LONDON

THE most striking thing about London—which is a wonderful place in scores of different ways—is its size. There are not many big hills in London, but if we were to stand on the top of a high building on Highgate Hill or, perhaps better still, if we go to the top of the tower of Westminster Cathedral or some other very tall building we can see London spread out beneath us and stretching out for miles in every direction, like a kind of frozen sea of brick and steel and concrete.

It is so large that it cannot just be called one city. In its very heart there are two cities—the City of London, which still occupies the area where London first grew up, and the City of Westminster, which includes the Houses of Parliament, the great departments of State, and Buckingham Palace, the London home of the King. But round about these cities stretch the other towns or boroughs: St Pancras, Kensington, Islington, Bermondsey, Chelsea, and many more, twenty-seven of them in all, which go to make up the County of London, in which about 4,000,000 people live. And still beyond the boundaries of the county London stretches out into Middlesex and Essex, into Kent and Surrey. More than 8,000,000 people live in the area of what is called Greater London, and the money that they pay to their local councils in rates runs into tens of millions of pounds. Almost one-fifth of the population of Great Britain lives in or near London, and one-quarter of the nation's trade is carried on in this area.

To some people it seems wrong that so many of Britain's people and so much of its wealth should be packed into this one great expanse of streets and buildings. To them London is an eyesore, an ugly, sprawling mass which ought never to have been allowed to grow to this size. But to other people the size of London is fascinating. They love its endless activity, the restless energy of its people, the thousands of cars and trams and buses, the trains which roar over the surface and under the ground day and night. It seems a kind of miracle that men could build a town, or collection of towns, over twenty miles across, and that they could make sure that all the millions who live there could be fed and carried to and from work each day. And sometimes people who think about London in this way, and who have grown to love it, find themselves wondering how it all came about. To find the answer to this we must make a journey into the past.

THE SITE OF LONDON

Let us try to imagine that we are making this journey into the past in stages. If we take away from London all the houses built since 1800 we find a startling difference in London's size. Instead of being over twenty miles across, it is only about four. It stretches from about a mile east of the Tower to the edge of Hyde Park. Northward it reaches the Euston Road, and in the south about as far as the Elephant and Castle. As we journey farther back into the past London grows smaller still, but the differences are never as great as between 1800 and 1950. Henry VIII's London is mostly inside the old City walls, and is not much over a mile from east to west. But we must still go back, for twelve hundred or fourteen hundred years, until the tramp of Roman sentries echoes along the battlements of those old walls, and a Roman forum stands in the middle of London.

The journey still is not finished. We must go back still farther until there is nothing on the ground where London is to be—just two small hills rising steeply from the broad and sluggish river Thames. The sounds of the city are gone. The roar of the twentieth-century motor-traffic, the clatter of eighteenth-century coach-wheels, the neighing of medieval pack-horses, and the tramp of the Roman sentry have died away. All is silence except for the cry of the birds in the reeds along the river and the sound of the wind rustling the trees and bushes that clothe the two little hills.

The top illustration at page 16 gives some idea of what this spot looked like at this time, nearly 2000 years ago, some little time after Jesus Christ was born. The ground is chiefly a kind of gravel with some soil called brick earth on top. Small streams run down to the Thames from the higher ground to the north and west, and these streams have cut the ground into two little hills.

The river running in on the west (or left of the picture) was a fairly fast stream. We do not know what name it had at this time, but later on it was called the river of Wells or the Fleet river (from the Anglo-Saxon 'fléot,' a place where vessels float). Its course is still marked by Farringdon Street. The river running between the two little hills came to be called Walbrook, and its mouth made a good harbour for small vessels. Perhaps it was already used for trading and fishing in a small way, but no one can be very sure. On the east was a depression which may originally have been a watercourse, and which later became part of the City ditch. It came to be called Shoreditch, a name which has been attached to this area ever since.

The two hills still exist, of course, though it is hard to see their shapes under the mass of buildings which cover them. The one to the west is Ludgate Hill, the one to the east is Cornhill. These names are on any map of London, and if we are Londoners we shall know them already.

At the water's edge the hard gravel formed a sort of small cliff, or bluff, of firm ground above the river. This was unusual, because the banks of the Thames for the most part were soft and marshy, lined with reeds and willow-trees, and with many little islands and sand-banks. The river ran slowly and with many windings through this soft ground, which was made up of silt which the river had carried down, when in flood, from the hills to the west.

THE SITE OF WESTMINSTER

So much for the site of London itself. The plate facing p. 16 shows the site of London—the two little hills and the little village which may have grown up there. In the picture below the same two hills appear in the top right corner. But two miles away on the left is a triangular piece of land which is practically an island. The two little creeks, or backwaters, run backward towards the spot where Buckingham Palace now stands, and one of them is joined by a stream which was later called Tyburn, and which ran from somewhere near where Marble Arch now stands. The Thames was very shallow just here, and there was a ford across the river. The island was suitable for people to live on, and it seems likely that a little village existed. Six or seven hundred years later, when Christianity had come to England, a small abbey was built and a few monks lived their simple life in God's service on this lonely island called Thorney. Much later still, when this first abbey was falling into ruin, the pious King Edward the Confessor began to build a new abbey, which was called Westminster. In the picture the two spots where London and Westminster were to grow up look small and lonely, and so, indeed, they must have been, covered with bushes and small trees, with just a patch cleared for cultivation here and there. Most likely the few people who lived there relied more on fishing and the snaring of birds and animals for their food than on farming, and did not have much to do with the big tribes living farther inland.

The top illustration at page 17 shows how dense forest came down close to these sites on both sides of the river, and even the land which looks fairly clear must be imagined as a sort of jungle of hazel and hawthorn bramble, with only rare patches of heathland here and there.

The London Basin

This picture shows clearly the major part of the course of the river Thames, which acted as a great highway into the centre of England. We can see how a great many rivers drain into the Thames from north and south. This country, which is drained by the Thames, from the Chiltern Hills, in the north-west, to the North Downs, in the south, is called the London Basin. If we were to cut this part of the Thames Valley in half downward we should be able to study the nature of the soil and rock of which it is composed. In the bottom illustration at page 17 this has been done, and the nature of the topmost layers has also been shown. Most of the London Basin is formed of clay soil (shown black in the diagram) with terraces of gravel scattered about on top (these are shown as light grey patches). The section shows that the clay is fairly deep, while the gravels are only thinly spread on top. Beneath the clay is a thick bed of chalk, which lies in a great fold, running from the Chiltern Hills to the North Downs. On the Downs we have only to cut through the grass for a few inches to find the chalk. Thus the whole basin is, as the name suggests, a kind of huge bowl or trough, with chalk at the bottom and on the rims, clay resting on top of the chalk, and gravel patches scattered on the clay. The river finds its way through a flood-plain in the lowest part of the Basin.

The gravel terraces were most important for the future growth of London and the towns and villages round about, for they were the parts most suitable for human settlement. There were no large trees on the gravel to be cut down, and the undergrowth was not thick and tangled as it was on the clay soil. In winter the gravel did not become heavy and waterlogged, like the clay, and so it was suitable for building houses. Because the rain-water collecting in the gravel could not drain away through the clay springs of clear drinking-water were usually found there, and the future site of London had many of these. Names such as Brideswell, Clerkenwell, St Chad's Well (Chadwell), Bagnigge Wells, and Sadler's Wells still mark places in or near the City of London, and are the medieval names of some of these old springs.

THE CELTIC PEOPLE OF BRITAIN

But in the far-off times before the Roman Conquest not many people lived in the Thames Valley at all. For thousands of years the peoples who lived in Britain had lived mostly on the slopes of the hills, for the low-lying ground was covered almost everywhere with dense forest, and the river valleys were mostly damp and marshy. In South-east England the trackways which served these peoples as roads ran across the country from the northeast to the south-west, following the course of the Chiltern Hills and the Mendips towards Avebury and Stonehenge, or came from the east along the North and South Downs towards the same spots. The settlements which did exist along the river in the Thames Valley were more or less isolated because of the difficulty of communication.

The people who lived in the south and east of England at this time, soon after the birth of Jesus Christ, were called Celts. They had come across the English Channel from Europe in large numbers at various times during the last hundred years before the birth of Christ. They were tall, fair-haired people with blue eyes, skilled at making tools and weapons of war from iron. They knew how to farm the land and keep cows and sheep; they could weave cloth, and the things they made from clay and metal were often beautiful as well as useful. Altogether they had reached a rather higher stage of civilization than any people that had yet come into Britain. They were also a warrior race, much cleverer at fighting than the short dark-haired people then in Britain. So they were able to push their way over a great part of Britain, conquering the inhabitants and becoming their

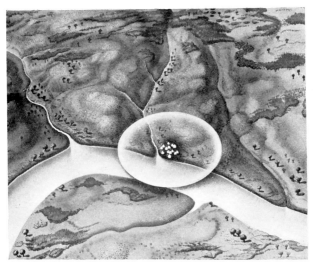

THE ORIGINAL SITE OF LONDON

The centre stream, Walbrook, enters the Thames between Ludgate Hill and Cornhill. The little British village which may have existed in pre-Roman times is shown.

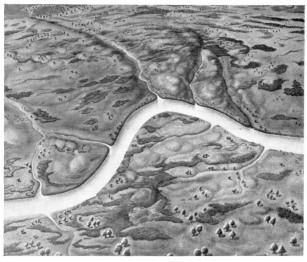

THE TWIN SITES OF LONDON AND WESTMINSTER

Both illustrations by courtesy of G.-B. Instructional, Ltd

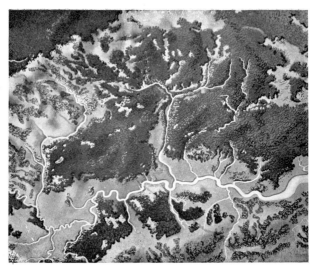

AN IMPRESSION OF THE DENSE FORESTS OF THE LONDON
BASIN ABOUT THE TIME OF THE ROMAN INVASION

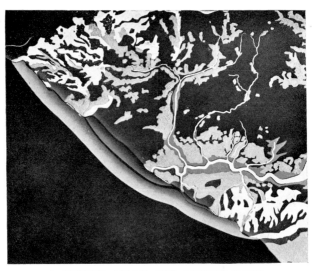

A SECTION ACROSS THE LONDON BASIN

The light grey patches represent gravels scattered on the black London
clay. Beneath the clay runs a belt of chalk which rises to the surface
on the high ground in the north and south (white patches).

Both illustrations by courtesy of G.-B. Instructional, Ltd

masters. The Celts who lived in the South-east of England are sometimes called Belgic peoples, from the tribe called the Belgæ, which was one of the largest. They are also called Iron Age people, because they knew how to make things of iron.

Although these people of the Iron Age were more skilled in agriculture than those whom they had conquered, so that they had begun to clear some of the forest and to drain some of the marshland, they still continued for the most part to inhabit the uplands, on which the Bronze Age people had lived before them. So it is that most of them lived well away from the Thames Valley, although they must have used the river a great deal as a highway. Their chief townships were at Camulodunum (just outside Colchester), at Verulamium (which is beside St Albans), and at Calleva Atrebatum (which is near Silchester, in Hampshire). These are the names the Romans gave to these places when they came finally to conquer Britain, in A.D. 43. They are probably the nearest the Romans could get to the Celtic or British names which the inhabitants used.

We must not confuse this Roman invasion in A.D. 43 with the earlier raids of Julius Cæsar, in 55 and 54 B.C. Cæsar's raids into Britain were only intended to stop the tribes from helping the tribes in France, which was then the Roman province of Gaul. Cæsar was having trouble with the tribes in Gaul, and he crossed into Britain to fight the tribe called Catuvellauni. For almost a century after his coming the British were left in peace, and during this time they prospered and began to trade with Roman merchants coming from Gaul.

In the fifth year of our era Cymbeline, of whom Shakespeare wrote, began to reign over the tribe called Catuvellauni. He increased their power over the other Celtic tribes in the south of England so much that the coins which he struck in his royal mint bore the legend "Rex Brittonum" (King of the Britons). Thus a British king used a Latin title, which shows that the influence of Roman ways of life in this part of Britain was grow-

B

ing strong. Cymbeline kept on good terms with the Roman emperors, encouraged their traders and craftsmen to settle here, and made his chiefs learn the Latin language. He could not have realized that all this peaceful penetration by the Romans would only make it easier for them to seize the country when the time was ripe.

Cymbeline reigned until A.D. 40, and during his reign the capital was moved from Verulamium to Camulodunum. Perhaps this was because the King wanted to be close to a port, for the Roman power and Roman trade were becoming very important to his kingdom. It is possible that during his reign a small trading-site may have sprung up on the site of London, but we cannot be sure about this. If there were such a place it must have been unimportant, for it did not have good communications with the places where most people lived.

THE COMING OF THE ROMANS

Three years after the death of Cymbeline the Romans struck in force. Ships carrying four legions sailed from the neighbourhood of Boulogne and landed at Richborough, in Kent. The Isle of Thanet was then a real island with a channel, called the Wantsum, between it and the mainland. It is possible that Roman ships passed through this channel and along the coast towards the Thames Estuary. But the army marched along the coastal strip to the north of the Wealden Forest. Striking across the Medway, they advanced to the Thames, and after a pause to await the arrival of the Emperor Claudius, who had come from Rome to take part in the campaign, they crossed the Thames at an unknown point, and advanced on Camulodunum.

Cymbeline's son Caradoc, whom the Romans called Caractacus, was then King. His leadership of the Britons in their fight against the Romans was so brave that many legends still survive about him; but the capital was taken, and Caradoc fled inland to fight in vain against the Roman legions which spread out over the land and conquered it.

The Romans regarded Britain as lying very nearly at the end of the world. As they advanced farther each year towards the north and west the country and the people grew wilder and more savage. This land of forest and rough hills, of cloud and rain and cold, must have seemed savage indeed, but the wild tribesmen with their old-fashioned war-chariots were no match for the tough, well-trained Roman soldiers—nothing could stop their advance. In order to hold down the conquered country the Romans needed forts and watch-towers linked up by good roads. Britain had hardly any good roads, only the winding trackways along the flanks of hills. So before long the hills and the valleys rang to the sound of axe and hammer as the Romans set foresters and surveyors and road-builders to work, driving wide, hard roads through forests and across rivers as they ran straight on over hill and dale for hundreds of miles.

Thus the mark of a Roman province was stamped upon Britain, the network of roads and armed outposts linking up the great fortified camps. By means of these roads the Romans kept a firm hold on the conquered country, sending messages, civil servants, and tax-gatherers to and fro, and moving troops swiftly to any place where trouble threatened. The roads had another use—they encouraged the growth of trade and the exchange of goods. With soldiers to keep the peace, trade began to increase.

Of course the Roman road system developed most quickly in the south-east of England, which was nearest to Roman Europe. To see why the Romans built their roads just where they did we have to try to put ourselves in their place. They were interested in moving troops and settlers into the island from Europe. Therefore they were interested in finding easy ways into England. The estuary of the Thames was one very easy route; the track along the North Downs between the Wealden Forest and the river was another. Both these routes led to the centre of the London Basin. Another natural route into South-east England was by way of the inlets of the Sussex and Hampshire coast, especially the waterways behind the Isle of Wight leading to Southampton water, and then along the Hampshire Downs and round the western end of the Weald into the London Basin. From the London Basin various routes led across the Chilterns into the English Plain. There was also the very important route along the Thames Valley and through the Goring Gap into the Midlands, and another route north-eastward from the London Basin towards the country of the Iceni.

Along all these routes Roman roads were built. They fanned out like the spokes of a wheel from the centre of the London Basin, the importance of which is obvious. Before they had gone very far with their road-building programme the Romans must have begun to think about finding a good point where they could join up their roads across the river Thames.

WHY ROMAN LONDON GREW UP

The spot they chose was to become the site of London. It was about thirty miles from the sea and was just about at the limit of navigation for small sea-going ships coming up with the tide. At this point the river swept close under the steep bluff before turning south-eastward in a deep bend. Hard ground overlooked the river. On the south bank opposite this point the ground was ten or fifteen feet higher than now and fairly firm. The whole place was easy to defend. It seemed a most suitable place for a bridge. No other place along the river offered the same advantages. So a trading-site was established on the easternmost of the two little hills, and a bridge must soon have been built. Perhaps it was at first a pontoon bridge, supported on heavy boats or rafts. But this must have been replaced by a bridge supported on timber piles.

LONDINIUM

This junction of road and river became an important trading centre. From the very first trade was its chief interest; Roman London was never a big military camp and it was never the official centre of government. The Romans called it "Londinium," which is obviously the Latin form of some Celtic word. There have been endless attempts to guess what the Celtic word was and what it meant. Some say it was Lyn-Den, which they translate as Lake City. Others have said it is Lun-Den, or Grove City. Still others think it may have meant Ludd's Fort, because the word 'Dun' in Celtic meant a hill or a fort. But no one can ever know the truth. The beginnings of London and of its name are obscure and likely to remain so, for the spot has been lived on now for over eighteen hundred years. In each succeeding generation some old buildings have been pulled down and the ground has been dug up to make room for new foundations, so that the relics of the past have been largely destroyed or built on.

At any rate Londinium was established some time between A.D. 43, when the Romans first settled, and A.D. 61, when Boadicea, Queen of the Iceni, who lived in Norfolk, revolted against the outrages and injustices of the Roman tax-gatherers and swept down with her warriors upon the city. Her followers sacked and burned London, and the ashes from the burning still lie a few feet beneath the City's streets, and are sometimes dug up in some fresh excavation. But soon the houses were rebuilt, and London flourished exceedingly. Ships sailed up the river on the strong tide, bearing supplies for the troops—wine and clothes and vessels of bronze and silver—all the luxuries of the ancient world for the Roman traders and their wives, for the officers of the legion and the government officials, and for the new ruling class of mixed Roman-British blood, which began to grow up. And to pay for these luxuries there came down the new Roman roads to London loads of hides and skins, tin, grain, pearls from the oyster-beds, and long lines of slaves.

The city spread from the eastern hill to the western hill, and among the wooden houses more imposing villas and temples of stone and brick arose. Some of these villas must have been very pleasant places, with beautiful gardens laid out with trees and, no doubt, fountains, which the Romans loved. There must have been a good deal of open space in the city and probably quite a few trees in public open spaces, so that the whole city had a spacious air about it. It grew so large and prosperous that somewhere about A.D. 120 the Romans began to build a wall all round it for protection.

This wall was a mighty affair, nearly 9 feet wide at the base, 20 feet or more in height, enclosing an area of about 330 acres, and measuring over 2000 yards across. It fixed the limits of the city for many centuries. In course of time, during the Middle Ages, the city limits extended to include clusters of buildings and large properties just outside the walls. Thus certain wards, such as Farringdon Without and Cripplegate Without, still have names which mean that these wards were 'without' the city wall—that is, outside the city wall.

The Roman wall was probably pierced by six gates. The names they were given in medieval times are all preserved in the names of places in everyday use to-day. On the west and nearest to the Thames stood Ludgate, on a hill above the Fleet river. Through this gate ran a road which came from Westminster or, perhaps, from farther west, from Brentford through Hammersmith, Kensington, Trafalgar Square, and the Strand. Next above Ludgate was Newgate. Through this gate ran the main road from the west, the Akeman Way, which was joined, just about where Marble Arch now stands, by the northern branch of Watling Street, the great road running to Chester. The next gate was Cripplegate; and the next after that Bishopsgate, through which ran the great road to York, called Ermine Street. Next to Bishopsgate came Aldgate and the road to Colchester, one of the chief cities of Roman Britain. Finally, from the bridgehead across the river in Southwark ran Stane

Street, which linked London to Chichester, and from this road forked the southern part of Watling Street, which we now call the Dover Road. Thus as early as the second century the bridge, the wall, the main gates, and the main roads, which were to provide the chief elements in London's structure for the next fifteen hundred years, were all in being.

The great area enclosed by the wall made London one of the largest cities of Roman Europe. On the top of the eastern hill, where Leadenhall Market now stands, was a building called the basilica, which formed one side of London's forum, or public meeting-place. This basilica, which served as the law courts and also as a business exchange, was a huge building over 420 feet long. Sometimes the pattern of human affairs is more lasting than brick and stone, as in this case, where a public market still does business where this Roman exchange once stood. In the same way, the barracks of the Roman soldiers stationed in London stood on or fairly near the place where William the Conqueror built the Tower of London for his soldiers, and it is said that a temple to Diana stood where St Paul's Cathedral was built. Once a place has been devoted to a certain purpose it seems that men like to go on using it for the same sorts of things indefinitely. The top illustration facing page 32 is a model of Roman London showing the chief gates and the roads through, as well as the other places that have been mentioned. It is interesting to compare this with a present-day map of the same area.

The Romans sometimes gave their cities titles as well as ordinary names, and in the fourth century London became Londinium Augusta. This was a grand title indeed. The Emperor himself was addressed as "August Cæsar"; so London's title had a royal ring about it. This helps us to realize what a very important place it had become. A mint was established there, and London was also by this time the seat of a bishop, for Christianity was coming into Britain. Commercially London was by far the most important city in Britain, though it was never the official centre of government.

THE DECLINE OF ROMAN BRITAIN

For three centuries and a half the Romans ruled Britain, and on the whole this was a good and prosperous time for the people in their charge. Roman rule was effective over the whole of England and parts of Wales, though the mountainous regions of Wales and Cumberland were not completely conquered. But there was always a certain difficulty in keeping Roman Britain free from the attacks of the Celtic barbarians. Hadrian's Wall, between England and Scotland, needed to be manned by picked troops always on the alert to keep out the Picts and Scots, and even before the end of the third century the garrison was driven back from the wall on one or two occasions. It was about the end of the third century that the raids of the Saxon and Frankish pirates became so bad that an officer called Carausius was given command of a fleet to patrol the English Channel and the North Sea in order to protect Britain. But Carausius used his position to seize power for himself, and became a kind of independent King of Britain. He managed to carry on in this fashion for about seven years. Eventually the Imperial Government reconquered Britain, and a new era of peace and prosperity began. But this incident showed how difficult it was for Rome to keep a firm grip on a province so far away, especially at a time when the Empire in the West was weakening.

Indeed, the years of Roman rule in Britain were numbered. The mighty Roman Empire, the most wonderful the world had ever seen, had begun to crack. At the centre the Imperial Government was no longer strong, and there were repeated attempts by would-be emperors to seize power in different parts of the Empire. In Northern and Eastern Europe the frontiers were under repeated attack by barbarian races who had not been conquered. In 330 the Emperor Constantine took the great step of building a new capital at Constantinople, so that the Empire soon ceased to be governed from Rome itself. To the dwellers in the countries round the Mediterranean it may have seemed that the stern, despotic, but successful rule of Constantine was bringing about a new age of greatness for the Empire. But for the people of Roman Britain, now civilized and peace-loving after so long a period of Roman rule, the outlook became alarming.

In 368 the first of a long series of disasters occurred. The Picts and Scots broke through the defences of the North and overran the country, looting, burning, and pillaging as far south as London. From this time onward life and property in Roman Britain were no longer safe. All over Europe the same sort of thing was happening. The Roman Empire in the West, torn by the private wars of rival emperors and armies, was unable to resist the enemies outside the frontiers.

For a time the Picts and Scots and other brigand tribes were pushed back, but the frontier defences were never properly repaired. The number of troops in Britain grew smaller and their quality poorer. In the west of Britain the Celtic culture began to revive, and these people, who had never completely yielded to the Romans nor adopted their ways, began to raid into Roman Britain from Wales and Scotland and Ireland. In the east of the island the Government was hard pressed to fend off the Saxon raids, which were increasing in strength.

Finally, another would-be emperor called Constantine withdrew the last of the army from Britain, in 407, to fight in his campaign against the true emperor, Honorius. From this time on it is doubtful if Britain was ever again garrisoned by Roman troops. The Germanic people were on the move all over Europe. In 410 Rome itself was taken by Alaric the Goth. In Britain the destruction of the Roman province, begun by the Celtic raiders from the north and west in the fourth century, was completed by the Saxon invaders of the fifth century.

The mixed Roman-British people, unfitted for war, were left defenceless by the crumbling of the Roman power. Their civilization was too frail to halt the fierce, warlike Angles and Saxons who fired their towns and butchered the inhabitants. The full horror of what happened in Britain in the fifth century is hidden from us, for the Saxons were thorough in their destruction. Some legends have come down to us, which seem to have started in these times, such as those of King Arthur. The tales of the old historian Gildas, written long after the event, give a faint, inaccurate picture. The rest is darkness—the darkness of the long night of the Dark Ages, which now descended over Europe. In this obscurity the fate of London too is lost for many years.

Chapter Two

THE DARK AGES: SAXON AND DANE

For more than a hundred and fifty years the fate of London is unknown. During this time the Anglo-Saxon raiders, no longer content to carry off plunder and slaves to their own country from Britain, began to conquer the land and to settle on it. Almost nothing is known of the details of this migration. It seems likely that bands of warriors came first, penetrating far inland up the rivers in their long-boats and then striking across country, beating down resistance, destroying towns and villages, killing and enslaving the inhabitants or sending them fleeing westward into the Lake District, Wales, and Cornwall. Later, perhaps, when they had conquered the eastern part of England, they sent back for their wives and children, and for other less warlike men willing to come and till the land in a country more attractive than their own. But we cannot be certain of any of this.

The Celtic peoples of the far west, who had themselves been waging war against the Roman power in Britain as it declined, looked down upon the Anglo-Saxons as pagans and barbarians and hated them bitterly. In their mountain strongholds they preserved the Celtic language and the Christian religion, but made no attempt to convert the invaders, against whom they fought fiercely. So the Saxon conquest took a long time to move from east to west across England, especially as the conquerors made no attempt to take advantage of the civilization which existed. There is hardly a single example of a Saxon settlement on the site of a Roman town. The conquerors preferred to destroy the towns and build their log-hut settlements in places of their own choosing.

Roman London falls into Decay

Yet London, almost certainly, was not destroyed. It was well placed for defence, surrounded by a stout wall, and had many inhabitants. So for a long time it survived the invasions. The Anglo-Saxon war-parties seem to have passed to north or south of it, penetrating farther into England while giving London a wide berth. In this way the city would have been cut off from the rest of the country, and this is probably what happened. Its trade grew less, and life for its inhabitants more and more insecure. So gradually people left London, slipping away, perhaps, to Brittany or to Wales and Cornwall. London became a haunted place, its streets half deserted, its buildings half ruined. The public services established by the Romans fell away. The marble columns of the temples cracked and fell. The lovely tessellated pavements of the rich villas sank beneath the untrodden dust that blew in through the empty doorways year after year. The conduits through which the little river Walbrook flowed under the Roman wall grew choked for lack of care. In course of time this produced a great marsh to the north outside the wall. The water even seeped under the wall into London itself. This marsh outside the walls became known in medieval times as Moorfields, and for centuries it was an evil place, a dumping-ground for all kinds of rubbish, until it was drained and became an open space.

So for a long time London was left alone, a decayed and deserted town. But gradually some kind of order grew up out of the destruction and desolation that had come to Britain. The different tribes and chieftains of the Anglo-Saxons carved their dominions out of England and Southern Scotland, and during the sixth century a chain of Anglo-Saxon kingdoms grew up, stretching from Northumbria, in the north, to Wessex, in the south. As part of this process new life came to London, which now began to recover some of its old prosperity as trade and orderly life revived.

In A.D. 597 another event took place of the greatest importance to Saxon England and, indeed, to the England of later days. It was in this year that St Augustine landed in Kent, sent by Pope Gregory to bring Christianity back to England. Before long St Augustine had founded an abbey at Canterbury and converted Ethelbert, King of Kent. Thus Kent, already the most civilized of Saxon kingdoms, became a firm basis for the spread of the Gospel over pagan England. But its progress was not fast. In 604 Augustine consecrated Mellitus as Bishop of London, which was now a place of importance once more, inhabited by the Middle Saxons, an offshoot of the East Saxons, who came to regard London as their capital. About 610, the Bishop Mellitus and King Ethelbert, the overlord of Sebert, King of Essex, began to build the first Christian church to stand on the site of St Paul's. But the citizens of London were not ready to receive the Gospel, and a few years later, having now grown powerful enough to be partly independent of the little kingdoms round them, they expelled the Christian missionaries. Thus it was that Canterbury, and not London, became the seat of the Archbishop.

SAXON LONDON REGAINS IMPORTANCE

By the seventh century, then, London had regained a great deal of its old importance. Just as it had been the most important city of Roman Britain, it was now the most important city of Saxon England. The natural advantages of its position at the "gateway of England" enabled it to survive misfortune. And misfortunes in plenty were to come! For a time, although the Anglo-Saxons were always a fierce and warlike people, often falling out among themselves, some progress was made towards national unity and a more civilized way of life. In this the Christian priests played no small part, establishing monasteries wherever their teaching had taken root, and teaching a new respect for life, a gentler code of manners, and some reverence for learning.

During this time London's importance continued to increase. In 730 the Northumbrian scholar and historian Bede speaks of it as "the mart of many nations by sea and land." But we have still no way of telling how much of the old Roman London had been reoccupied by the Saxons. No doubt Lundenburh, as they called it, was the largest town in England, but among a people who did not really dwell in towns we cannot have any clear idea what this means. Then, towards the end of the eighth century, the Saxons, who now lived in scattered hamlets and farmsteads on their clearings in the forest and had forgotten their bold, sea-faring ways, received a rude shock.

THE COMING OF THE VIKINGS

Once more the sea-raiders came over the North Sea to Britain, and the Anglo-Saxons, who had taken the land from the Roman-British, now had to fight for their farms and houses against the Vikings of Denmark and Norway. For fifty years, from about 797 to 850, the Vikings raided Britain and the coast of France, secure in the knowledge that there was no sea-power to stop them, and carrying back to their homes the gold and jewels of monasteries and churches, and tales of the fat fields and rich meadows over the seas. Then in the later half of the ninth century these bands of sea-warriors, enlisted under many separate chieftains, learned to operate as armies under a single commander, and the conquest of England and of that part of France called Normandy began in earnest. The Danes won from the Saxons a whole great territory called the Danelaw, stretching from Lancashire and Yorkshire into Essex, and but for Alfred the Great, who became King of Wessex in 871, they might indeed have conquered all.

Alfred was only twenty-two, but he was a great soldier and a great leader of men. Under him the Saxon resistance stiffened and the Danes were held. During these desperate times London, which must have seemed a rich prize to the Danes, suffered grievously. In 839 the city was attacked, and there was a great loss of life within the walls. In 851 or thereabouts London was again stormed and captured for a time. In the winter of 872, after a summer spent in fierce warfare against Alfred and the men of Wessex, the Viking army retired to London to shelter behind its walls during the months of wet and cold. When Alfred finally forced the Danes to make peace a few years later he managed to secure London for Wessex, although it was very near the frontier of the Danelaw, from which the Norsemen could not be dislodged.

ALFRED FORTIFIES LONDON

London, which guarded the entrance to the Thames Valley, was the key to Alfred's kingdom. He realized its great importance, and in 886 he fortified the city, rebuilding or repairing its ancient walls and encouraging more people to settle there. The tradition of independence and self-defence against aggressors, which London built up during the years of trouble, remained active for many centuries. Right through the Middle Ages and into the seventeenth century the citizens of London were ready to take up arms in their own defence if need be, and were quick to resist any threat to the independence which the city won for itself in its long history.

For twenty years after the Treaty of Wedmore, in 878, Alfred prevented the Danelaw from growing larger; indeed, he even managed to make it smaller. He beat off fresh Danish raids from across the seas, he encouraged the spread of Christianity, and he even found time to foster the growth of literature and learning, for he himself loved scholarship. He strengthened Wessex by building a fleet, improving the army, and building a sound system of government. The Norsemen who had settled in the East of England made no such progress.

THE FIRST KINGS OF ENGLAND

So it was that when Alfred, truly called the "Great," died, in
A.D. 900, his son Edward the Elder and his grandson Athelstan
were at last able to reconquer the Danelaw. The Norsemen were
never driven out, but they accepted the English as overlords,
and these two kings were the first who can truly be called Kings
of England. So for a time there was peace of a sort in England,
though it was never quite complete. The great Viking war-
parties setting out in their long-boats from Norway and Denmark came less frequently. The whole movement lost its force
for a while, and for almost a hundred years London busied itself
with trade and forgot the battle-cries of the Norsemen, which
the citizens had come to know so well.

But towards the end of the tenth century there came to sit on
the throne of England an unhappy king, so unfit to govern that
he has gone down in history as Ethelred the Redeless, or
Ethelred the Unready. In his reign the terror from the North
overshadowed England once more. The Vikings were on the
war-path again, and this time the prize was not the golden
candlesticks of a few monasteries or a few hundred acres of
English land—it was the Kingdom of England itself. Nevertheless there was money enough to be had, for the weak Ethelred
raised and paid over to the invaders huge sums as Danegeld, a
kind of ransom repeatedly paid in the hope of staving off defeat
and conquest.

LONDON LEADS RESISTANCE AGAINST FRESH DANISH ATTACKS

In these new Danish wars the part played by London was
outstanding. The leadership and rallying to resistance, which
should have come from the King, came rather from the citizens
of London. So it is not surprising that the city now became one
of the chief targets of the Viking attacks. Though not the official

ROMAN LONDON

The wall was built about A.D. 120. Note the rectangular street-plan, the bridge, the basilica and forum on the top of Cornhill, and the barracks on the site of the Tower.

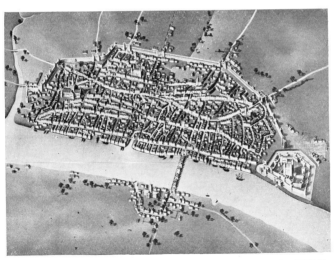

LONDON ABOUT THE END OF THE FIFTEENTH CENTURY

This was on the eve of the first great expansion.

Both illustrations by courtesy of G.-B. Instructional, Ltd

A RECONSTRUCTION OF CHEAPSIDE ABOUT 1600

Gold and silver plate and other luxuries were sold there, while food and other necessities could be bought in the side-streets.

WHAT A LONDON WHARF PROBABLY LOOKED LIKE ABOUT THE END OF THE FIFTEENTH CENTURY

Both illustrations by courtesy of G.-B. Instructional, Ltd

capital of England, London, because of the power and wealth it had built up, and because of its readiness to defend itself, was the real heart of England. In 982 the city was captured and burned. But it did not die. The Vikings could not hold the city. London 'carried on.'

This final war of conquest against England was led by Sweyn Forkbeard, the fierce King of the Danes, and in 994 he personally led another attack against London, but this was beaten off. There were many stories told of the desperate attempts made during this war to bring down this stronghold of English resistance. On one occasion the Danes tried to get above the city, but were halted by defenders posted on London Bridge. The Danes actually dug a canal round the southern end of the bridge through Southwark and got their ships through. But the city did not fall. According to another story, another set of assailants decided to destroy London Bridge by using ropes made fast to their ships to pull down the piers of the bridge.

London received Sweyn Forkbeard at last, but in peace, for Ethelred fled into exile and Sweyn was King of England for a year. In 1014 he died, and Ethelred returned. But in 1016 Ethelred also died, and the war began again. Canute, the son of Sweyn, claimed the throne and was chosen by the Saxon Witan, an assembly of bishops, earls, and royal officials, at Southampton. But London chose Edmund Ironside, the son of Ethelred, and such was the city's power that, with London's support, Edmund was able to wage war for seven months against Canute. But at the end of that time Edmund died, and Canute became King of England and of Denmark.

LONDON PROSPERS UNDER CANUTE

During his long and wise reign London, which had put up such a fierce resistance to the Danish king, prospered exceedingly because of him. Many Danish merchants came to London, and

C

the city shared in the international trade which was being built up in Northern Europe by these energetic and adventurous merchants. For the first time since the days of the Roman peace London became again not only the most powerful place in England, but an important city in European trade. These Danish colonies in London have left their mark in the names of churches dedicated to the Scandinavian St Olaf, or Olave, and in the name of the Church of St Clement Danes, in the Strand.

By the time Canute died the Saxon and Scandinavian peoples settled in England were ceasing to be distinct, and the formation of the English nation was well under way. The Scandinavian empire of Canute did not long survive his death, and in 1042 the Saxon line was restored to the throne of England in the person of Edward the Confessor. By this time, as we have said, London had left the bad years behind it and was again a proud and prosperous city, though not so beautiful as it must have been six centuries or so before, under the Romans.

EDWARD THE CONFESSOR AND THE BEGINNING OF WESTMINSTER

London, however, was not the official capital of England. So far as there was one, the capital was Winchester. Nevertheless, it is in Edward's reign that the little island of Thorney begins to acquire some importance. Edward built himself a palace of some sort on the island and near by began to build the great church which, with many alterations and additions, has come to be known as Westminster Abbey. It is not certain whether he first built his palace so as to be near London or whether he built it so as to be able to supervise the building of the Abbey. His reason for building the Abbey is said to have been in consequence of a vow that he had made. Edward was a very pious man, and he had vowed to make a pilgrimage to Rome. But he found himself unable to do so, and to make up for this he said that he would build a new St Peter's Church upon Thorney

Island. And a great and splendid building it was! When the saintly king died he was buried in the church, and his tomb became a shrine which was a place of pilgrimage for centuries afterwards. It is in the Abbey to-day, one of the most ancient of the many precious relics and monuments in that wonderful church.

But before he died King Edward had helped to pave the way for a great change in the life of England, and of London. Though he was the last of a great Saxon line, Edward was strongly influenced by the manners and customs of the Normans, among whom he had spent his youth. He admired their ways, and surrounded himself with Norman noblemen at his Court. He encouraged trade with Normandy and allowed their merchants to come to London. He gave high places in the Church to Norman bishops and put Norman earls in charge of important fortresses. Thus he prepared the way for the coming of the Normans under Duke William, who conquered England in 1066.

Chapter Three

NORMAN AND MEDIEVAL LONDON:
THE KINGS COME TO WESTMINSTER

THE events of September and October 1066 are so well known that there is hardly any need to tell again how King Harold, the son of Earl Godwin of Wessex, having defeated the forces of Harold Hardrada at the battle of Stamford Bridge, in Yorkshire, had to march south in haste to meet the long-expected invasion of William of Normandy. But what perhaps is not so well known is that Harold and his army spent six days in London, resting and refitting, and that when they marched out again to the place in Sussex called Battle a unit of Londoners went with them. They were led by a high official of the city called Ansgar the Staller, and at the battle of Hastings they fought well. They did more. They survived the battle and withdrew towards London, taking their wounded commander with them. And London looked to its defences.

Once he had defeated Harold, William's main anxiety was to secure London. Not only was this powerful place the key to the kingdom, but William was anxious to improve the doubtful legality of his claim to the throne by having London recognize him formally as King of England. He therefore advanced without delay through Kent and approached the southern end of London Bridge. As his army drew near William sent out a force of cavalry to try out the defences of the city. But the Normans found Ansgar and his men waiting for them, and though the Londoners were driven back and Southwark, as we now call it, was sent up in flames, the defenders held fast on London Bridge.

William was too good a general to be tempted into sitting down for a long siege. He swept on along the south side of the Thames, destroying villages as he went, until he came to Wallingford, where he crossed the Thames and turned north, still destroying what lay in his path.

So at last William the Conqueror came to Berkhamsted, to the north-west of London, in Hertfordshire. From this position he could threaten London and prevent help reaching her from the rest of England. In any case, there was little spirit of resistance left in Southern England, and the old capital at Winchester had already surrendered.

So William's policy was successful. After a few week's hesitation, and a brave but futile attempt to recognize the boy Edgar Atheling as King, London sent a deputation to William which acknowledged him as King and invited him to be crowned in the great church that Edward the Confessor had built on Thorney Island.

WESTMINSTER GAINS IMPORTANCE UNDER THE NORMAN KINGS

Henceforth this little patch of ground two miles to the west of London begins to take its name from this great church or 'minster,' which came to be called Westminster, the minster in the west. The accident of Edward the Confessor's pious resolve to build a palace and an abbey here had great consequences. Instead of living in London or elsewhere in the country, as the Saxon kings seem to have done, the Norman kings tended to regard the palace at Westminster as their chief home, although they too moved about a great deal. The power of London was too great for even the King to be able to neglect it for too long, yet on the other hand it probably did not seem wise for a Norman king actually to live within the city. So Westminster with its palace seemed a convenient place. The Conqueror's son William Rufus added a great hall to the palace. The building was altered and improved by Richard II and has come down to us as Westminster Hall. As time went by other buildings grew round the palace and the abbey to house the king's officers and his courts of law. The old capital at Winchester lost more and more of its importance as the centre of government shifted to Westminster.

NORMAN LONDON

As for London itself, we have already said that it had recaptured most of its old importance and bore no resemblance to the deserted, ruinous city of five hundred years before. But to us it would have seemed a strange mixture of busy seaport and country town.

The ships of many nations could be seen at anchor in the Pool of London, below the bridge, or were tied up along the wharves. There was a small harbour, or tidal basin, at Billingsgate, below the bridge. Above the bridge was a harbour called Dowgate, at the mouth of the Walbrook, and another which the Saxons called Edredshithe, and which was later known as Queenhithe. The old wooden bridge had a drawbridge in it through which ships could pass, and smaller boats could attempt the risky business of shooting between the great piers of the bridge, which took up so much room that the water ran like a millrace.

But inside the city itself ran a maze of narrow, twisting streets which had grown up during Saxon times. Many of them still follow their same course on the ground in the City of London to this day, and for this reason the City is a difficult place for modern traffic. These narrow streets were lined with wooden houses. Because of the destruction that London had suffered in Saxon and Danish times, nothing was left of the many fine buildings of Roman times, and even the regular lay-out of their streets had disappeared.

Though the population of the city was numerous, we must not be misled by some old chronicles which gave an exaggerated idea of its numbers. Even in the time of Richard II, long after the times with which we are dealing, the population seems not to have been above 40,000. Norman London was probably rather less than this. So there was still room for many open spaces, especially in the northern part of the city between Broad Street and Basinghall Street, on either side of the Walbrook. Perhaps this area was still too damp and marshy from the effects of the silting-up which had occurred in earlier times. Other open spaces were occupied by two great markets, one in the eastern half of the city, called Eastcheap, which lay midway between the present Thames Street and Fenchurch Street, and another in the west, called Westcheap, which afterwards became known as Cheapside. This was the chief market of the city. It stretched more or less from the walls of St Paul's Cathedral, which crowned Ludgate Hill, half-way across the city to a little bridge which crossed the Walbrook. It was lined with booths and sheds, where merchants sold their wares and where craftsmen of various kinds followed their trades.

In many of the great markets of the cities of the Middle East or the Far East merchants and craftsmen of different callings tend to gather together in the same part of the market, so that one alley is called the Street of the Silversmiths, another the Street of the Shoemakers, and so on. So it was in the old market in London. There is still a Cheapside in the City, and a very important street it is, lined with great banks and office buildings, which would seem like fortresses to the merchants of Norman times, and the streets off Cheapside still have such names as Ironmonger Lane, Wood Street, Milk Street, Bread Street, Friday Street (where fish for eating on Fridays was sold), Sopers Lane (where the soap-sellers stood), and so on. These names tell us of the trades that were carried on in these parts when they were just unpaved lanes among the mass of booths that stood in Westcheap. At page 39 there is a picture of what Cheapside was like much later on, towards the end of the fifteenth century.

A Description of London under Henry II

No one has written anything which has come down to us describing what London was like in the time of William the Conqueror or his son, but we do possess a most vivid description of what London was like in the reign of Henry II—say, about the year 1170. The chief difference between London at that time and the London of a hundred years earlier was that most of its Saxon churches and other relics of London's Saxon period had been destroyed in a great fire which swept London in 1135 and was almost as disastrous in its effect as the other great fire, of 1666. As the city was rebuilt after this fire many more buildings than before were built of stone, but for all that it was still for the most part a place of wooden houses, and remained so for many centuries.

¶ London.

Brute & his men wente forthe and
sawe about in dyuers places/ whe
re that they myght fynde a good place &
couenable/ that they myght make a cy-
te for hym & for his folke. And so at the
laste they came by a fayre Ryuer þ is called Tamys/ & there Brute began to bu-
ylde a fayre Cyte/and lette calle it newe
Troy/in mynde & remembraunce of the

One of the Earliest Views
of London, showing the
Tower and St Paul's

The most imposing of London's buildings must have been the Tower of London itself, though the great church of St Paul's, which was being rebuilt for the third time after being twice destroyed by fire, was destined to be one of the wonders of its time. But certainly at the end of the twelfth century there was nothing in London to rival the great fortress which the Conqueror had begun by building the White Tower, and which his descendants were continually enlarging and strengthening. On the western side of the City, near the present Blackfriars Bridge, was another fortress also built by the Conqueror, called Baynard's Castle, after Ralf Baynard, its Norman lord. To the north of this, and nearer to Ludgate Circus, there was probably another and smaller Norman fortress, called the Tower of Montfichet. These powerful places probably served a double purpose. They guarded London from the east and from the west, and made it much more able to resist attack. As it was now one of the most precious possessions of the new Norman Kings of England, this was obviously a wise precaution to which none could object. But the castles also gave the Conqueror and his descendants powerful strongpoints within the city, in case there should ever be need to put down revolt among its proud and independent citizens.

As has been said, we have a wonderful picture of life in London in the reign of King Henry II, and from it we can imagine pretty well what London must have seemed like at practically any time in the twelfth century and probably for a good time after that as well. This account of London comes to us in the form of a prologue to the life of St Thomas, the murdered Archbishop of Canterbury, and it is written by William Fitzstephen, a monk, who was, as he says, a fellow-citizen of St Thomas, "his clerk and a member of his household." Fitzstephen calls himself a fellow-citizen of the Archbishop because both were Londoners by birth, and he describes the city, its people, and its buildings.

One of the most remarkable things about London even at this early date was the great number of its churches. Fitzstephen says that there were in London and the suburbs—that is, in he small built-up areas just outside the walls—thirteen large churches belonging to monasteries, and a hundred and twenty-six parish churches. London must have been full of the sound of bells all day long.

In these suburbs, he says, are the gardens of the citizens who dwell there, spacious and beautiful, and dotted with trees. On the north side of the city, outside the walls, were grazing-lands and cornfields, watered by pleasant streams and dotted with water-mills, whose wheels were pleasant to the ear. Beyond this, says Fitzstephen, stretched a great forest, which was perhaps Epping Forest. Here were the dens of many kinds of beasts—deer, wild boars, and wild bulls. The citizens of London were fond of hunting and had hunting rights in Middlesex and Hertfordshire, in all the Chiltern country, and in Kent as far as the river Cray.

Within the city those who followed various trades, those who sold different kinds of goods, and those who hired themselves out for different kinds of labour were found each day in their proper places according to their work. Fitzstephen also says that there was in the city a public cook-shop. It seems rather odd that there should be only one for so large a city. Perhaps he means to say that there was a street of cook-shops. Here cooked meats, fish, and poultry could be bought, and this was evidently thought to be a notable convenience. This is how he describes the place:

There is in London upon the River's Bank a public Place of Cookery, among the Wines to be sold in the Ships, and in the Wine Cellars. There every Day you may call for any Dish of Meat, roast, fried, or boiled; Fish both small and great; ordinary Flesh for the poorer Sort, and more dainty for the Rich, as Venison and Fowl. If Friends come upon a Sudden, wearied with Travel, to a Citizen's House, and they are loth to wait for curious Preparations and Dressings of fresh Meat; let the Servants give them Water to wash, and Bread to stay their Stomach, and in the mean Time, they run to the Waterside, where all Things that can be desired are at Hand. Whatsoever Multitude of Soldiers, or other Strangers, enter into the City, at any Hour of the Day or Night, or else are about to depart; they may turn in, bate here, refresh themselves to their Content, and so avoid long Fasting, and not go away without their Dinner. If any desire to fit their dainty Tooth, they take a Goose; they need not to long for the Fowl of Africa, no, nor the rare Godwit of Ionia. This is the public Cookery, and very convenient for the State of a City, and belongs to it. Hence it is, we read in Plato's *Gorgias*, that next to the Physician's Art is the Trade of Cooks, and Image and Flattery of the fourth Part of a City.

Fitzstephen has only two criticisms of the city: "The only plagues of London are immoderate drinking of idle fellows and often fires."

On the sixth day of every week there was a horse-fair and market on the "smooth field" outside the city walls. The name is preserved in Smithfield, and there is still a great market there to this day—London's great meat-market. In Henry II's reign not only were horses bought and sold here, but races were also held.

Fitzstephen has a lot to say about the sports of the young men of the city. In the summer they practised archery, ran races, jumped, and wrestled. And the maidens danced to the sound of the lute when the moon had risen. At Easter the young men went on the river in boats and tilted with lances at a target made fast to a pole in the middle of the river. A dangerous sport this, for if the lance did not break they were thrown into the water and the boat swept past them. There were three schools in London, just three, so we can imagine that not many boys went to school at all. But each year on Shrove Tuesday those that were at school brought with them their fighting cocks and held cock-fights in the schoolroom! And each school seems to have had its own particular kind of ball-game, as did most of the separate trades. In winter the boys and the young men skated upon the ice. Usually they went to Moorfields, for this was still a great marsh, which was often frozen over in the winter-time.

There were no steel skates in those days, and Fitzstephen says that the skaters tied the leg-bones of certain animals beneath their feet and then pushed themselves along the ice with iron-shod poles. So the young men of London, of every class, seem to have been an active, merry, courageous lot of people who made the most of their opportunities for amusement and lived a busy, turbulent life in the midst of their rich city.

And rich it certainly was by now. In addition to its merchants and its craftsmen, Fitzstephen adds that nearly all the bishops, abbots, and noblemen of England kept town-houses in London "and thither they do often resort and lay out a great deal of money: and are called into the City to consultation and solemn meetings, either by their King or their Metropolitan or drawn by their own affairs." Thus we see that at this early date London had already the power to act as a sort of magnet, drawing to itself all those with important business to transact. This centralizing power of London in the affairs of the nation has continued to be a notable characteristic of London right up to our own times and has helped much to encourage its growth.

We have mentioned the frequent fires which were a constant hazard of life in London. This was not surprising in a city that was still very largely built of wood and where the houses were sometimes roofed with thatch, although regulations against this practice were made at a fairly early date in the Middle Ages. The constant risk of fire prompted the city authorities to issue frequent orders to ensure that houses with upper storeys had ladders to use in case of fire and barrels of water in readiness beside the front door. It was also provided that strong iron crooks, chains, and strong ropes should be kept in readiness at certain spots; these were for pulling down blazing houses in order to prevent fires from spreading. In the great fire of 1135 London Bridge itself shared the fate which sooner or later overtook most of old London's great buildings—it was utterly destroyed.

London Bridge rebuilt in Stone

The loss of the bridge was a disaster, and efforts were made to rebuild it immediately. Perhaps the result was not altogether satisfactory, or perhaps the disaster to the bridge set some one thinking, but, whatever the cause, one man, at any rate, conceived the idea of building a bridge entirely of stone. This was thirty or so years after the fire of 1135, and the man who carried through this tremendous enterprise was an obscure chaplain of a small church in the Poultry, called Colechurch. The priest's name was Peter, and so he is known as Peter de Colechurch. The building of so great a bridge, over 900 feet long and 30 or more feet in width, with nineteen arches and a drawbridge, must have made great demands on the building and engineering skill of the times. London's river was wide, the current was fast, and the tides strong—the unknown elements in the task must have been immense. But the work went forward. Money was contributed by the citizens, by the people of England, by the kings. In 1176 building began, it went on for more than thirty years, and long before it was finished Peter de Colechurch lay in his grave. But at last it was finished, and there was probably no other bridge like it in the whole of Europe at that time, perhaps not in the whole world. It lasted for 650 years and became a symbol of the endurance of London and its institutions; it became part of the very history of England.

By about the year 1210 the bridge was finished, and by about this time also the boundaries of the city had extended outside the city walls to the limits still to be found on modern maps, marking the limits of the City of London to-day. On all the main roads coming into London these limits were marked by a gate or bar, and the most famous of these is Temple Bar, in Fleet Street. Where it stood it is still the custom of the Lord Mayor to meet the King when he makes a visit to the City. It is curious that, although the great area of London has spread out for miles in all directions from these old boundaries, the City itself has never made any real effort to extend its legal authority beyond the limits laid down seven hundred years ago.

By this time, too, the great Cathedral of St Paul's, though not complete, was largely rebuilt, and dominated the western part of the city just as the Tower dominated the eastern part. This huge building was nearly a hundred feet longer than the one we know to-day, and, of course, totally different in style. Its spire soared up to almost 600 feet and must have been a glorious sight. It was served by about two hundred clergy, to say nothing of scores of lesser officials, each with his staff and servants. If one adds in the carpenters, masons, and the like, the number of people dependent on the Cathedral for a living must have run into many hundreds.

LONDON RELIGIOUS FOUNDATIONS

Every religious foundation was run on the same open-handed scale, and in medieval London there were thirteen large monastic establishments besides the many parish churches and the fifty or so ecclesiastical inns. Throughout all England at this time the power and wealth of the Church were enormous, and London was no exception. A very large part of the city was owned directly or indirectly by the Church—some put the figure at more than half. Within the walls, running from the east through the north of London to the west, were the Priory of Crutched, or Crossed, Friars; then Holy Trinity; then St Helen's Priory; Austin Friars; St Martin's le Grand; Grey Friars; Christ's Hospital, where the Bluecoat boys first went to school; and the House of Dominicans, or Black Friars. Many of these names will be familiar to all who live in London. They are preserved in the names of churches originally built by these great religious houses or in the names given to the localities where they once stood. But all of them in medieval times were large establishments with many monks or nuns and other dependants. All of them owned much property both within the city and just outside it, and none of this property could be sold.

Outside the city walls were many other religious houses, each owning many broad acres, so that the Church lands surrounded London like a girdle. To the west, south of the Strand, were the White Friars; to the north-west, in Smithfield, stood the priories of St Bartholomew and St John; and north of St Bartholomew's (whose name lives on in the famous hospital of that name) stood the great house of the Carthusian monks, the Charterhouse, some relics of which still survive in Charterhouse Square. Outside

Bishopsgate were two religious hospitals, and south of the river stood the great hospital of St Thomas and the Abbey of Bermondsey.

A great deal of this land owned by the Church was kept as pasture- and farm-land; in addition Moorfields remained a marsh right up to 1605. Thus most of the land round London was out of reach for the builder until the Reformation and the dissolution of the monasteries. Gradually all land which was available for building was used up, and the city became more and more tightly packed as time went on. The houses also grew taller as old ones of one or two storeys were pulled down and replaced with three- and four-storeyed houses. Other devices were adopted to make the most of every inch of space, such as building out the upper storeys of a house so that they projected over the lower storeys. In narrow streets the top storeys of houses opposite one another were often nearly touching. At page 32 is a picture which tries to give an idea of what London may have looked like by the end of the fifteenth century.

Gradually as time slipped by, as one century slid into another, the bad old days of war and destruction faded from memory. The city increased steadily in power and prosperity. Life was settled and, by the standards of those days, secure. Not that we should have found London a peaceful city by our standards. It was a turbulent place, and men were still given to settling their quarrels by resort to arms. There was no police force as we know it, and the citizens themselves had to keep order in their own districts. It was also a very noisy place and a very dirty one. Heavy wagons and pack-horses clattered over cobbles with tremendous din or churned the side-alleys into a mass of ruts and pot-holes. Runnels or gutters ran down the middle of each street, and were used to carry away all kinds of slops and evil-smelling matter. Other rubbish was deposited in stalls at the end of each street which were cleared at intervals (not too regular) by public carts. But, nevertheless, life in London was organized according to certain public regulations, and as time went on a strong city government grew up. It fought hard to win its privileges from the kings of England, and already by 1192 London had elected its first Lord Mayor, Henry Fitz-Ailwyn. But before we can understand how London was then governed we must say a little about the craft and merchant guilds which controlled London's trade.

THE CITY GUILDS

The idea of forming guilds or associations of men who came together for certain purposes was a very early one in London's history. Indeed, the earliest guilds were not confined to London. At first these guilds seem to have been partly religious in character. A number of men would form a society to maintain an altar to some particular saint and to see that Masses were said in his honour, and so on. But the society usually had other purposes as well. In an age when life was uncertain and misfortune was frequent the guilds fulfilled many of the functions which insurance societies now carry out. By collecting subscriptions from members the guilds built up funds for helping members who were sick or had lost employment or who needed money for the burial of a relative. Such societies required that their members should be good and sober citizens.

Gradually the guilds tended to become organized on a trade basis. Members of the same trade or of the same craft would band together for their mutual protection. The guilds laid down certain rules about trade practices, insisted on certain standards of honesty and fair dealing in trade, and continued as before to build up funds with which to look after those members who needed help. The formation of such trade guilds seems to have begun in the twelfth century.

During the fourteenth century the growth of these guilds, or city companies, went on at a great rate. Certain very important results emerged from this great movement to organize the trade and the workers of London. The merchant class strengthened its position in the affairs of the city. The merchant guilds, or companies, were dominated by the rich and powerful merchants who owned large enterprises, and these guilds were able to wield more influence than the purely craft guilds, composed of more humble citizens, who had only their own skill.

Thus twelve companies came to be known as the Great Companies; these were the Mercers, Grocers, Drapers, Fishmongers, Skinners, Merchant Taylors, Haberdashers, Salters, Ironmongers, Vintners, and Clockworkers, and, in addition, one true craft guild, the Goldsmiths. These merchant companies were at the height of their power by the fifteenth century.

London's Self-government

The guilds modified London's system of self-government without destroying it. During the long centuries of struggle for independence London had worked out a democratic way of running public affairs. From the old folkmoot, or town meeting, which used to meet in the open near St Paul's, there had grown up a system electing a Common Council, a Court of Aldermen, two Sheriffs, and a Lord Mayor. Many charters from many kings had confirmed this system and given London special privileges. But from 1375 or thereabouts the members of the Common Council were no longer elected by the citizens of the wards into which the city was divided, but by the trading guilds, and especially the craft guilds. As for the Great Companies, it gradually became their exclusive right to provide the members of the Court of Aldermen, and through them the Sheriffs and the Lord Mayor.

Thus the government of the city was controlled by the same hands that guided its fortunes in trade. By the fifteenth century this development in the organization of the life of the city through the guilds was complete, and the shape of things thus laid down survived for centuries. Even to-day the broad outline remains

D

the same. Although there have been modifications in the system of election to bring it into line with modern practice, the City Companies still retain great power in the affairs of the City, though they have long since ceased to be merchant companies trading in the goods from which they took their names.

TRADE IN THE FIFTEENTH CENTURY

But in the fifteenth century they ruled the city from the fine new Guildhall, which occupied the same site just off Cheapside

A HUNTING-PARTY IN THE FIFTEENTH CENTURY
From Wynkyn de Worde's "Boke of Hawkynge" (1490)

on which the Guildhall of to-day still stands, and from the warehouses along the river they sent out to Europe goods of all kinds and especially corn and the wool and cloth which were England's chief wealth. In return they brought into London the fine and costly goods of distant lands: gold, silks and furs, sugar and rice, coffee and spice, and indigo—things which added a little richness and luxury to life in days when living was rough even for the wealthiest. The illustration at page 33 shows the kind of ships the merchants used. Note also the small tidal docks and the cranes that were used in those days.

By this time English ships were beginning to be built in great numbers, and the English people, who had for a long time forgotten their seafaring ancestors and had become a nation of farmers and shepherds, were beginning to find their sea-legs again. Nevertheless the trade of London was still carried largely in foreign ships—that is, ships from Europe, and Britain as a whole still looked inward towards Europe. The great con- federacy of German trading cities which was known as the Hanseatic League had close trade connexions with London. The League had a house in London called the Steelyard, which stood close to the shore just under the present Cannon Street Station, and from this headquarters the League controlled all trade between London and Germany and the Baltic. Other ships traded to the Low Countries, and Venetian galleys even made the long trip from Venice, which at that time dominated the Mediterranean because of its great trading power.

Compared to the wealthy and powerful states of Europe, with their great cities and air of cultured civilization, England was a small country of rude peasants and uncouth nobles. Its one city of international importance was London.

The Fifetenth-century World and Britain's Position

The world of those days was a little place compared to the one we know. Europe was its centre; beyond, to the east, lay the vast plains of Russia, stretching out to fabled and unknown lands where the Mongols and the Tartars roamed the borders of the Empire of China, the legendary land of far Cathay. To the south lay the coasts of Africa, the ancient lands of Egypt and

Mesopotamia, and the land of the infidel Turk, where once Jesus Christ had lived and taught and where Imperial Rome had ruled. Through these lands led caravan routes to India, which few white men had ever seen. But something of the treasures and the craftsmanship of that far-off region filtered through the channels of trade even as far as London.

The British Isles themselves seemed to lie almost on the edge of this medieval world. Beyond were the mists and fog, the storms and perils of the Atlantic Ocean. What lay out there no man knew. To most people it seemed self-evident that if any-one were foolhardy enough to set sail to the west, and lucky enough to survive the dangers, he would only end by sailing clean off the edge of the world into some unthinkable abyss.

THE RENAISSANCE

But times were changing fast. Something very wonderful and very hard to describe was happening in the minds of men at this time. In Europe and the Near East a great struggle had gone on for centuries to fill the gap caused by the breakdown of the Roman Empire. The Roman system had many faults, some of them monstrous ones, but at its best it had brought peace, prosperity, and security to millions of people. It produced men of great wisdom, whose teachings were of value to the whole human race; it had encouraged tolerance in religious belief, it had produced the greatest literature of ancient times; it had fostered the love of art and beauty, of gracious and ordered living.

In the chaos of the Dark Ages most of these things had been lost. The feudal society of the Middle Ages, though more secure, was still limited in outlook, narrow-minded, war-like, and sus-picious, each little state striving against its neighbours for its own advantages, knowing and caring little of what took place beyond its own small circle. The one great unifying influence and the one great guardian of wisdom and learning was the medieval Church.

But in the fifteenth and sixteenth centuries much of the writing of Greece and Rome which had been lost to Europe for a thousand years and more began to be rediscovered. Manuscripts began to reach Italy which had lain forgotten in the libraries of Alexandria and Constantinople. Scholars began to study these, as well as the writings of Arabian scholars who had never quite lost touch with the learning of the ancient world, and who had themselves made great contributions to the science of medicine and mathematics, and to philosophy. A new light of scholarship began to dawn in Europe, and the Church ceased to have the sole control over what men read and thought. It was as though a veil was lifted from the minds of educated men, and a great new spirit of inquiry possessed them.

This spirit spread through every kind of human activity. Science began to make some progress after having lain stagnant for centuries, invention was quickened, the new device of printing made enormous strides, books began to be in great demand, scholars in different countries corresponded, advances were made in navigation; the new freedom in men's minds produced a totally new and modern type of literature; painting and sculpture returned to the ancient world for their inspiration and produced, not slavish copies, but great masterpieces employing new technique. Everywhere there was a spirit of inquiry, experiment, and adventure. In religious matters the authority of the Church was questioned and the great movement which we call the Reformation began. The advances in astronomy, mathematics, and navigation prompted a great series of explorations and voyages which changed, in a few years, the whole face of the known world. In these wonderful times there was indeed a Renaissance, a rebirth, in the minds of men and in the fortunes of the world.

Out of all these many currents which were active at the time we may take two—the Reformation and the voyages of discovery—and say that these, above all, were charged with great significance for England and for London.

Chapter Four

TUDOR LONDON: THE GROWTH BEGINS

THE DISSOLUTION OF THE MONASTERIES

BY the sixteenth century the liberal forces which we have described in Chapter III were in full flood and their influence was felt in many ways. One striking fact about sixteenth-century Europe was that the different states now began to be clearly distinct, and to think of themselves as nations. Italy was still a collection of small principalities whose frontiers might change according to the fortunes of war, and the same was true for parts of Germany; nevertheless, the kingdoms of Naples, Portugal, Spain, France, England, Prussia, and the hard core of the territories of the Emperor in Central Europe were well-established sovereign states which were to endure for centuries. Men began to think of themselves as Englishmen, Frenchmen, Spaniards, and so on. The medieval world was left behind. Most of the kings and princes of Europe at this time were very nearly absolute rulers—that is, they had for the most part hardly any parliaments or councils with power to restrain them in the way they chose to govern.

In these circumstances the former power which the Pope had possessed over the rulers of European states grew weaker as the new nationalism grew stronger. His power was further weakened by the strong criticism of the Church's established teaching which had spread through many parts of Europe. Many people were in favour of this movement for reform in the Church, and it gained great support. It arose out of the new freedom to question and to criticize existing ways of thinking and acting which is a characteristic of the Renaissance. The kings and princes found that they could not stay out of this question of the Reformation of the Church whether they wanted to or not, and the whole question became entangled in the complicated web of European politics. Many of Europe's rulers became identified with the new 'Protestant' Church movements which sprang up in various countries.

In England this question became mixed up with the quarrel of Henry VIII and the Pope over the affair of Henry's divorce from Katherine of Aragon. The upshot of it was that Henry broke with the Pope and set up a new form of Catholic Church in England. Many subsequent acts affecting the Church flowed from this great decision. The one that interests us most, because it was one that had great consequences for the growth of London, was Henry's decision to dissolve the monasteries and to dispose of their great holdings of land and property.

Holy Trinity Priory, in Aldgate, was the first monastery in England which Henry dissolved upon his own authority. Soon afterwards he moved more boldly, sweeping away the rest of the monasteries in London and in the rest of the country. These fine religious houses and their land and property were granted to various noblemen and knights whom Henry wished to reward, or were sold to wealthy people as a speculation on which they might make a profit. Holy Trinity itself, for instance, was pulled down and sold for building material by Sir Thomas Audley. The Church of the Crutched Friars became a carpenter's shop and a tennis-court. Even the parish churches which were allowed to remain lost all their ancient glories. To emphasize the break with the past and the establishment of a new, simpler, more severe style of worship, the fonts were defaced, the altars stripped of their fine cloths, the walls, once painted with bright colours and pictures of stories from the Bible, were white-washed. The priest put off his gorgeous robes and preached in a plain black cassock. Not all of this, of course, was done by the King's order. Very many people felt that it was right that the

Church should become poorer, that the monasteries should go, and that the ritual and doctrine of the Church should be reformed.

Church Property in London and Westminster changes Hands

In London and Westminster this seizure and disposal of Church property meant that a great amount of land changed hands. In Westminster the Crown itself took over certain property, which resulted in an extension of this "royal city." York House, the great town-house of Wolsey, the Archbishop of York and Henry's chief Minister until his fall, stood in what we now call Whitehall. Henry took this property and turned it into the beginnings of the great palace of Whitehall. In St James's Fields was a religious hospital, once a place of isolation for lepers. This Henry turned into a hunting-lodge, and later added to it, until it became the Palace of St James. Along the Strand the bishops, bereft of much of their wealth and power, quietly left their great town-houses, which were taken over by great earls—Dorset, Essex, Arundel, and the like. Somerset House still stands on the site of the house occupied by the Lord Protector Somerset in the reign of Edward VI, and Northumberland Avenue, near Charing Cross, runs over the site of Northumberland House, which existed until the nineteenth century. Of course these great changes did not take place overnight. They went on all through the reign of Henry VIII and in the reign of Edward VI. Gradually speculators bought up the wide Church lands and the fine gardens, pulled down the old buildings, parcelled the ground up into building lots, and constructed smaller houses which they put up for sale.

By the second half of the sixteenth century—say, in the early years of the reign of Queen Elizabeth—the face of London had changed a great deal. By this time, too, there are beginning to be good maps, on which we can actually see what London looked like at this time.

London expands beyond the Walls

One of the earliest maps is that drawn by Ralph Agas showing London as it was about 1560, and from this we can see that at that date, although the city was expanding, there were still open spaces within the city walls. East Smithfield was still a large field; there were gardens and trees and open spaces in Aldgate. Christ's Hospital, the Blue Coat School founded upon the site of Grey Friars Priory, still had a big garden stretching to the city wall. But houses were beginning to stretch out east along the road to Whitechapel through Houndsditch, from Aldgate as far as Bishopsgate, and north along the road out of Bishopsgate towards Shoreditch Church. There were houses with gardens in Moorfields and the district now called Finsbury. Farther west, round the Church of St Giles's Cripplegate, a suburb was beginning to grow up, and there were many houses in Smithfield outside the walls. More houses stretched out along Holborn, which took its name from the Oldbourn or Turnmill Brook, a tributary of the Fleet river. Along the Strand were the great houses we have mentioned, linking London to Westminster, where the new palaces obtained by Henry VIII had now become the permanent centre of the life of the court. The illustrations at page 64 are from a model of Elizabethan London which shows the actual buildings in detail.

As the sixteenth century went on and the reign of Elizabeth grew longer London prospered, and the demand for land and for new houses increased. So within and without the city building went on, and, despite the efforts of Elizabeth's councils to control the growth of London, expansion continued almost without check, to the east, to the north, and to the west and north-west. There was also a sizeable suburb growing up south of the river in Southwark and Bankside. There had always been a suburb of sorts south of the river round the end of the bridge, but in the sixteenth century this began to grow larger. This was partly because Bankside became a kind of entertainments centre for

London. There were strict regulations in the city against the showing of plays and public entertainments because of the dangers of infectious disease being spread by large crowds, and because of the fear that large crowds might become unruly. So bull-and bear-baiting pits sprang up in Bankside, and the Globe Theatre was built there. There were also pleasure gardens as well as other entertainments a great deal less respectable.

John Evelyn, in his diary, describes a visit to a fair in Southwark in 1660:

BEAR-BAITING

From a woodcut in the 'Anti-Bossicon,' by William Lily and William Horman (1521)

I saw in Southwark at St Margaret's faire, monkies and apes dance and do other feates of activity on the high rope; they were gallantly clad *à la mode*, went upright, saluted the company, bowing and pulling off their hatts; they saluted one another with as good a grace as if instructed by a dauncing-master; they turn'd heels over head with a basket having eggs in it, without breaking any; also with lighted candles in their hands and on their heads without extinguishing them, and with vessells of water without spilling a drop. I also saw an Italian wench daunce and performe all the tricks on the high rope to admiration; all the Court went to see her. Likewise here was a man who tooke up a piece of iron cannon of about 400 lb. weight with the haire of his head onely.

LONDON'S INCREASE OF PROSPERITY IN THE SIXTEENTH CENTURY

This prosperity of London in the later part of the sixteenth century was part of a general increase in the well-being of England as a whole. There was peace in England, and for large numbers of people a freedom from poverty which had never been known before. For most people there was reasonable freedom of thought and worship, and for a time politics did not trouble the ordinary man and woman. It was, as Trevelyan says, "the golden age of England." Trade was increasing rapidly, and though the volume of trade carried on inside the country was far greater than that done with foreign countries, nevertheless overseas trade was also rapidly expanding. The cloth trade, which had stood still for a time in the fifteenth century, was now once again one of the mainstays of British export trade, and most of this went to long-established markets in the Low Countries, especially in Antwerp. But fundamental changes were taking place in the position of Great Britain in the world which were not slow in having their effect on London's trade and on the activities of her merchants.

THE VOYAGES OF DISCOVERY

These changes had their origin in the bold voyages of ocean explorers which had begun more than fifty years before. We have described already something of the idea that men had of the world they lived in up to about the end of the fifteenth century, and we have tried to show how the Renaissance, by freeing men's minds and giving them a new desire to find out more about the world, had encouraged progress in science, navigation, and the like. One of the established beliefs that was questioned was that the earth was the centre of the solar system. Another was the equally old belief that the earth was flat. As mathematics, astronomy, and navigation made progress, an increasing number of people began to believe that the earth was round. They thought that there must be vast oceans which no one from the Old World had ever seen, and that it might be possible to sail upon these oceans, in the stout new ships that were then being built, to new lands beyond the seas, or else to discover new sea-ways to India and China, which had always been approached by land after long and arduous journeys.

So the sailors began to explore the high seas. The Portuguese led the way in the fifteenth century, sailing down the coast of Africa as far as Cape Verde, then pushing out into the Atlantic until they found the Canary Islands and the Azores. About the year 1483 a certain Genoese sailor, Christopher Columbus, tried to persuade King John of Portugal to fit out an expedition to sail across the Atlantic. Columbus had made voyages in the Atlantic, and had been as far as Iceland. He believed that it was possible to reach Japan (which was supposed to be rich in gold) by sailing westward round the world. Columbus failed to persuade King John, and so he took his proposals to the Court of Spain. Not until 1492 did Columbus succeed in getting his ships from the Spanish King and then only one was a fully decked ship, and that of no more than a hundred tons. The other two were just large open boats of about fifty tons. In these perilous craft Columbus discovered the new world of the Americas.

Great excitement was caused in Western Europe by the news of his voyages. The Portuguese had already succeeded in finding the way round the Cape of Good Hope, at the tip of Africa, for this had been done by Diaz about 1486. Now, in 1497, they dispatched Vasco da Gama, who succeeded in rounding the Cape of Good Hope and sailing up the east coast of Africa to Zanzibar. From here, with the help of Arab seamen, he struck across the Indian Ocean to the west coast of India. In the same year another Genoese sailor, Cabot, sailed from Bristol and discovered Newfoundland and the coast of Labrador. So the veils of ignorance were rolled back, and a vast new horizon dawned upon the world. In 1519 began the most wonderful of all these early voyages of discovery. Five ships, with two hundred and eighty men, under the command of a Portuguese captain, Magellan, set out from Spain, and sailed west and south along the coast of South America. The southern tip of the American continent is a dark and cheerless land of fog and cold and tempest, but Magellan found his way through the tortuous and forbidding channel which is named after him, the Strait of Magellan, and came at last into the Pacific Ocean. For ninety-eight days the expedition sailed on into the unknown across this huge expanse of empty sea. Imagine what resolution, what leadership, what faith in God must have been needed to keep these men sailing westward! The water in their casks was a green slime, their bread and meat crawling with maggots and weevils, their bodies rotted with the scurvy which beset every crew deprived of fresh vegetables on a long voyage. At last they reached the Philippines, and here Magellan himself was killed in a fight with natives and several of his captains murdered. The remnants of the expedition sailed on somehow, and in 1522 one ship, with eighteen men aboard, sailed up the Guadalquivir river to the anchorage at Seville, whence the five ships had set out. A sad and terrible outcome of a great enterprise, but that one ship had sailed right round the world, and so the voyage which had killed Magellan and so many other brave men had brought the last and ultimate proof that the world was round, and that the ships and men of the sixteenth century could sail upon its oceans to all its continents. The sea-ways of the world were open, and along them trade would flow faster and in greater volume than ever it could by the overland routes of the Old World.

A REVOLUTION IN GREAT BRITAIN'S POSITION

By the time of Elizabeth the effects of the discovery of the new world across the Atlantic and of the sea-ways to Africa and the Far East were being felt in Britain. Instead of looking inward to Europe Britain was beginning to look outward over the oceans, and was beginning to discover her destiny as a seafaring nation. The great change in the position of the British Isles in the world was beginning to be realized by the Queen's sailors. From being a group of islands almost on the edge of the known world the British Isles had actually come to be in a central and commanding position in the world, situated almost in the centre of the land hemisphere and better placed than almost any other European nation to develop sea communications all over the world.

During the reign of Queen Elizabeth I the commercial centre of the world shifted from Antwerp to London. The sea-power of the world ceased to centre on the Mediterranean—henceforth it was the prize to be won by those nations whose ships could sail the wide oceans and open up new areas of trade. The Spaniards, the Portuguese, the French, and the English fought for this prize, but the French soon dropped out of the struggle. It was left for Spain, Portugal, and England to fight it out. Off the coasts of Africa and India the English merchant ships often had to reply to Portuguese guns before they could make contact with the native peoples with whom they sought to trade. In the New World of the Americas English sailors looted the Spanish treasure ships and the rich Spanish colonies. Small, fast flotillas of ships under the inspired leadership of men like Francis Drake combined war against the greatest of England's enemies with private adventure and private profit, for these expeditions, though often carrying the Queen's blessing, were equipped at their own expense, and the profits or losses of the voyage were the private risk of their captains. It was fortunate for the survival of the British nation that the small handy ships of the English privateers, relying on superb seamanship and the fire-power of their guns, proved time and again to be more than a match for the great galleons and war-galleys of Spain, which were handled like floating platforms designed to bring their crowds of men-at-arms and archers into action. England was still the weakest of all the nations which clashed in this struggle for survival and for sea-power in the world, but in those breathless years of Elizabeth's reign her seamen and her shipbuilders evolved a new style of naval warfare which was to give her in time the greatest sea-power in the world.

THE MERCHANT ADVENTURERS

Yet we must not think that these activities on the high seas
were wholly or even mainly the affair of the Queen's Navy,
Despite the risks of attack from pirates or from jealous rivals.
armed merchant ships from England were opening up the new
sea-routes for trade, hoping for peaceful passage, but ready if
need be to fight their way through. Most of the capital risked

FLEET STREET BANK SIGNS

Left: the Three Squirrels (Gosling's Bank). *Right*: the
Marigold (Child's Bank).

in these ventures came from the City of London. During the
Queen's reign the merchant adventurers steadily acquired fresh
rights and powers. The privileges of the Hanseatic League in
London were abolished. The London merchants opened up their
own 'courts' or trading offices in Antwerp and Hamburg, and
at key-towns on the East Coast of England such as York, Hull,
and Newcastle. A long list of private companies, many under
Royal Charter, were set up to trade with various parts of the
world. For the Baltic there were the Eastland Company and the
Muscovy Company; for the Mediterranean the Levant Company. The Virginia Company was formed to develop the new

colony founded by Raleigh in America. In 1600 the great East India Company began to establish the trading depots in India which were to grow eventually into a great Eastern Empire under the British crown.

East of London, down-river in Stepney, Rotherhithe, and Deptford, there was much building of ships, and many of the merchants interested in these ships and their trading began to live in these parts. The Queen's interest in the Palace of Greenwich, at which she often stayed, also led to increased activity on this side of London. Gradually Greenwich became more and more associated with the affairs of the Royal Navy, which was still in its infancy at this time.

GRESHAM BUILDS THE ROYAL EXCHANGE

Within the City itself the opening of a notable new building reflected the increasing financial importance of London. This was Sir Thomas Gresham's Royal Exchange, opened by the Queen herself in 1570. To-day if we go by bus or Underground to the Mansion House, which is pretty well in the heart of the City, we shall find, if we stand with our backs to the Mansion House itself, that there is an open space across the road in front of us. At one side, to the left, is the Bank of England, and straight ahead, behind the open space, is the Royal Exchange. Of course, this is not the one that Gresham built, but it stands on the same site. Its position is almost symbolic—it is in the very centre of London, and Gresham's Royal Exchange came to occupy a position at the very centre of London's trading activities.

Let us try to understand why this was. Sir Thomas Gresham came of an old City family. His father and his uncle had both been Lord Mayors. So he was brought up in an atmosphere of trading and handling money and early proved himself very capable at these matters. When still quite a young man he was

A MODEL OF ELIZABETHAN LONDON

Above: Southwark Cathedral, in the foreground; London Bridge, completely covered with houses; the Tower, in the background.

Below: The spires of Old St Paul's and of London's many churches reach towards the sky; in centre foreground is the Globe Theatre.

By courtesy of G.-B. Instructional, Ltd

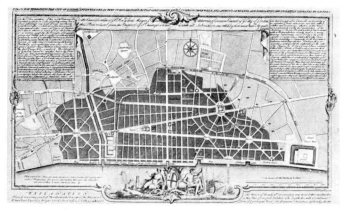

WREN'S PLAN FOR THE REBUILDING OF THE CITY

It is dignified and simple; a few spacious squares linked by broad main roads provide the framework. Other streets divide the rest of the area into rectangular blocks. To have carried out the plan one single authority would have had to control all the ground.

THE INDUSTRIOUS 'PRENTICE AS LORD MAYOR
William Hogarth

This illustrates the turbulent street-life of London in the eighteenth century.

made the Royal Agent at Antwerp. This was a post of great importance, for Antwerp was at that time the money centre of the world or, at any rate, of the Western World. For a long time it had been the custom for the English Government to raise the King's loans (by which it carried on the government of the country, while waiting for the taxes to come in) from the bankers and merchants of Antwerp. The Royal Agent had charge of the business connected with these loans. Sir Thomas Gresham served under Edward VI, Mary, and Elizabeth with great success, and was able to reduce the cost of raising these loans by large amounts. In Antwerp he learnt a great deal about the ways of carrying on business, and eventually he came back to London to put his ideas into practice. The Royal Exchange provided a centre where London's merchants and bankers could meet together, exchange information, carry out business, trade among themselves in different commodities, and arrange new ventures between themselves. Nowadays there are so many of these great markets and exchanges where dealers in stocks and shares, or in commodities of various kinds, can come together to do business and regulate their affairs, that we can hardly see how business could be carried out without them, but the Royal Exchange was the first great institution of this kind in London, and it is of the first importance. It led to a great development of enterprise, and London began to displace Antwerp as the money centre of Europe. A proof of this is that in time the Queen's loans were no longer raised in Antwerp, but were provided by the merchants of the City. Thus the interest on this money, which amounted to very large sums, was no longer sent out of the country, but was available in London to be used to increase business still further.

London helps to fight the Armada

So the city prospered and spread. The great threat from Spain was finally met in 1588, and London played its part. Thirty ships put out from London to help repel the Armada, and the London-trained bands got out their pikes and marched out to Tilbury to join the army which the Queen reviewed there and to which she made her famous speech: "I know I have the body of a weak and feeble woman, but I have the heart and stomach of a king, and of a King of England too." So the Armada broke before the muzzles of English guns, and England, led by the great Queen and sustained by the wealth of London, rolled forward towards the opening of a new century.

Early Stuart London

The houses spread out farther and farther beyond the walls, particularly towards the west, until by Early Stuart times they had reached St Giles-in-the-Fields and stood at the bottom of what we still call the Tottenham Court Road. Thus by about 1640 Holborn was lined with houses on both sides all the way to St Giles-in-the-Fields, and most of the land between here and the Strand was built up, though not of course so densely as it afterwards became. During this time Covent Garden was laid out as a residential area, in about 1631, and Leicester Fields was turned into a select square full of genteel houses a few years later. The creation of the 'West End' was under way, and a good deal of this new building was not only outside London's wall, but outside the boundaries of the City's authorities. But London did not seek any further extension of its boundaries or of its civic authority. Within its own limits the City was now very populous. Already at the time of Queen Elizabeth's death it is thought that it may have been over 200,000. During the next fifty years it increased still further.

Yet there was still space in London here and there. There were houses with gardens and courtyards and stables; the Corn-market was still a broad and open space; Cheapside was still double the width it is to-day. In the middle of Cheapside (or Chepe, as it was still called for the most part) stood one of the great crosses which marked where the body of Queen Eleanor, the wife of Edward I, rested on its journey to Westminster. There was another open space with less pleasant associations— that at Smithfield, where executions of criminals and heretics still took place. The great church of St Paul's still towered above the western half of the city, but had lost much of its former magnificence. The great spire had fallen down in 1561 and had never been replaced. Within St Paul's Churchyard, which was surrounded by a wall pierced with six gates, was an area crowded with stationers and booksellers' shops and planted with trees. This must have been a lively and pleasant spot. But inside the church only the chancel remained available for the worship of God. The rest of the huge building had become, by long custom, a public place for everyday affairs. There was a public thoroughfare through the transepts and across the church. Carters tramped through with goods on their backs. Pedlars offered their goods for sale. Certain spots in the church had become devoted to certain purposes. At one pillar stood servants waiting to be hired; at another were gathered clerks and scriveners ready for offers of work.

On the river an unending procession of small craft moved busily up and down, for this was still the great central highway of London. The roads were narrow and unpaved, often heavy with mud and deeply rutted. To travel in a heavy lumbering coach, without springs, say from Westminster to Greenwich, was a slow and uncomfortable business. Though coaches were slowly becoming more and more fashionable, many people still went on foot or on horseback. And many, whenever the journey allowed, took to the river for part of the way. People with business across the river used one of the regular ferries.

instead of going out of their way to cross London Bridge, which was still the only bridge. So the river was never empty. The State barges of royalty or of great personages glided by, brave with much gilding and silken awnings and fluttering pennants. Light craft of various sizes could be hired like taxis from the various 'stairs' or landing-stages along the banks, larger craft carrying a number of passengers made regular trips up and down the river like the water-buses and river-steamers of our own day. And on every tide the lighters moved to and fro between the shipping in the pool and the warehouses along the quays.

Henri Misson, a Frenchman, in a book entitled *Memoirs and Observations in his Travels over England, 1670–85*, left these notes about the boats that plied for hire on the Thames:

> The little Boats upon the Thames, which are only for carrying of Persons, are light and pretty; some are row'd but by one Man, other by two; the former are call'd Scullers, and the latter Oars. They are reckon'd at several Thousands; but tho' there are indeed a great many, I believe the Number is exaggerated. The City of London being very long, it is a great Conveniency to be able sometimes to make use of this Way of Carriage. You sit at your Ease upon Cushions, and have a Board to lean against; but generally they have no covering, unless a Cloth which the Watermen set up immediately, in case of Need, over a few Hoops; and sometimes you are wet to the Skin for all this. It is easy to conceive that the Oars go faster than the Sculls, and accordingly their Pay is double. You never have any Disputes with them; for you can go to no Part either of London, or the Country above or below it, but the rate is fix'd by Authority; every Thing is regulated and printed: The same is done with respect to Hackney-Coaches, and Carts for the Carriage of Goods.

But though there was water in plenty on which to row or sail, the citizens of London in the early seventeenth century were not well supplied with drinking-water. The population had increased to such an extent that the springs and wells, of which we have spoken earlier, were no longer really sufficient for the needs

of London and Westminster and the suburbs. Of course, improvements had been made. Lamb's Conduit Street, which may
be found on modern maps, a little to the north of High Holborn,
not far from the Great Ormond Street hospital, is a reminder of
William Lamb, a wealthy City man of the late sixteenth century
who collected the water from several springs to the north of this
new suburb (as it then was) and brought them, through over a
mile of lead pipe, to a conduit at this spot. But it was left to Sir
Hugh Myddleton to bring in, as a private commercial venture, a
great new supply of water which was to meet the needs of almost
the whole of London for over a hundred years. This he did by
cutting what was almost a new river, beginning at Chadwell
Springs, near the town of Ware, in Hertfordshire, and ending in
a reservoir at Islington. From here the water could be piped to
various points in London. This mighty enterprise was completed between the years 1608 and 1613.

The village of Islington, near which the New River Head was
dug, was a sizeable place. Other villages round London were
also growing: at Mile End and Bethnal Green and Hoxton, in
the east; at St Mary-le-Bone, Paddington, Brompton, and
Chelsea, in the west; at Vauxhall, Lambeth, Camberwell,
Newington Butts, Walworth, and Peckham, in the south.
Southwark was already a small town into which the village of
Bermondsey was being absorbed. Between the royal 'city' of
Westminster and the City of London itself there stretched a
built-up region as large as, or larger than, the old City within
the walls, from which it had sprung. The existence of this great
collection of houses and people dominated the surrounding
countryside. For many miles round the farmers concentrated on
market-gardening and dairy produce to supply this huge market.
The villages grew prosperous and began to grow into little
towns. Farther afield, all over England, the influence of this
Greater London was felt. Here was the Court; here was the seat
of Government; here were the Inns of Court, where one might
learn to practise law; here were the merchants and the bankers,

whose actions affected trade all over England; here was power; here was preferment. So London was like a magnet, drawing to itself all those who sought to make their way in the world. From now on, it seemed, nothing could stop its growth—and, indeed, nothing could, not even fire and pestilence on a scale that few great cities have ever experienced in time of peace.

Chapter Five

THE GREAT FIRE AND AFTER

INSANITARY CONDITIONS IN LONDON: OUTBREAKS OF PLAGUE

WE have talked a great deal in the previous chapters about the great qualities of the London of the past—its prosperity, its power over the trade and the political affairs of England, the vigour and energy of its citizens, the waves of new building which spread out round the old city. But there was a darker side to all this. Like every great city in the Middle Ages, and for centuries afterwards, London was often an unhealthy place to live in. To-day we take for granted the ceaseless care which is taken to guard the health of all who live in civilized countries like ours. The water that we drink is purified and filtered; beneath our houses and our cities are sewers to carry away all kinds of filth and foul water to places where it can be properly treated and rendered harmless; if some one is unfortunate enough to catch an infectious fever he can go to hospital to be made well again and to prevent the fever spreading; at all our ports there are quarantine regulations which prevent people or animals carrying infection from entering the country to spread disease. But in the seventeenth century hardly any of these safeguards existed. Through the middle of the narrow streets of old London ran open drains into which all manner of refuse was tipped. There was no main drainage for the houses; instead there were cesspools, which were emptied at irregular intervals. Sometimes the fluid from these cesspools seeped through the ground and poisoned the water in wells or springs near by.

Finally, this old London was still a town of wooden houses, and in such houses rats find it easy to live and breed. Many of these rats came from the ships that thronged the Port of London. They were covered with fleas and often infected with a dreadful deadly kind of fever called plague. The fleas helped to spread this fever among human beings. It is thought that this plague which often visited London was the same disease which had killed off almost half the population of England in the fourteenth century, and had been called the Black Death. There were violent outbreaks of plague in London in the late Middle Ages, but by the seventeenth century these outbreaks had become much rarer. Nevertheless, the old Bills of Mortality issued by each ward in the City, listing those who had died each week and the ills from which they had suffered, show that even when there had not been major outbreaks for a long time the plague still carried off a few here and there. In the reign of James I 30,000 people in London died of it. Then, after a quiet period, there was another bad attack, in the time of Charles I. After 1636 it died down again. Only those who studied the Bills of Mortality knew that the plague was still about, lying quiet like a sleeping beast, biding its time before it went tearing and ravaging through the City once more. But the years passed and the people forgot—until the year 1665, a year which London will never forget.

THE YEAR OF THE GREAT PLAGUE

For four months in the early part of this fateful year there had been no rain, so that the dust and smells of the City were even worse than usual by the month of May. Then reports began to circulate that the plague was increasing quickly in the quarters round the City. By June 10, according to Samuel Pepys, the famous diarist, it had struck in the City itself. By June 23 it had become dangerous to hire a hackney coach, for fear that such a public vehicle might carry the infection. By June 29 Pepys reports that the courtyard at Whitehall was full of wagons and people ready to leave the town. The mortality bill had risen to 267, and it seems that many of these deaths were at the West-minster end of London. By July 13 the number for the week was 700; by July 27 the number was 1700. So the pestilence mounted week by week. On August 10 the bill was "above 4000 in all, and of them above 3000 of the plague." On August 31 over 6000. Terror spread among the inhabitants. All who could do so fled from London, and because many were already infected the plague spread to the towns and villages round about.

Inside London the rule was that when a house was visited by the plague it was at once shut up and marked with a cross upon the door. None might come out and none might go in. Despair was locked in with the desperate inhabitants of such houses, for often entire families lay ill at the same time, and there was nobody to nurse them. Even if doctors could be found brave enough to venture into such houses it was of little use, and before long there were whole districts in which not a doctor or an apothecary remained alive. People dropped and died in the streets, and their bodies were picked up by the death-carts which went round the streets, collecting bodies from the houses and burying them in great common graves. By September the plague had reached its height. On the 20th of this month Pepys wrote in his diary: "The whole general number [for the week] is 8297, and of them the plague 7165." He had been to Lambeth and he writes: "But Lord! what a sad time it is to see no boats upon the river; and grass grows all up and down White Hall court and nobody but poor wretches in the streets." Again, on October 16, he writes: "I walked to the Tower; but Lord! how empty the streets are and melancholy, so many poor sick people in the streets full of sores; and so many sad stories overheard as I walk, everybody talking of this dead, and that man sick, and so many in this place and so many in that."

Slowly, as the weather grew colder, the fury of the plague

lessened. The bills of mortality grew shorter, yet still with a sudden increase now and then. By the turn of the year London began to resume something of its normal life. Yet still the plague dragged on into the new year, never quite disappearing, though the weekly number of deaths from it might sink as low as thirty. But the streets filled up, and the trade of the City began to flow again with something like its old vigour. London began to be herself again.

But a worse blow than even the plague was to befall her. The last traces of the pestilence were to be purged from the city by fire—and, with the plague, a great part of London's wealth and almost all her ancient and historic buildings were also to be consumed.

THE GREAT FIRE OF LONDON

On Sunday, September 2, 1666, a fire broke out in the house of the King's baker, one Faryner, who lived in Pudding Lane, Thames Street, near London Bridge. No uncommon thing this—fires were frequent among the old wooden houses, and usually they did not spread very far. But this time it seemed as though the Fates had decided to make sure that the fire would spread. The baker's house seems to have been full of kindling and fuel for his oven fires. The houses all round that area were densely packed. They were nearly all of wood, covered with pitch on the outside. The district contained many warehouses for storing goods from the ships on the river near by. Many of them were full of things that would burn well, such as brandy, wine, oil, silk and cotton goods, and the like. The fire broke out in the early morning, about two or three o'clock. All over London people saw the glare in the sky. By breakfast-time it was said that 300 houses had been burned down. The end of London Bridge was alight, and a wide area on both sides of the north end of the bridge.

Again Pepys paints the picture for us. He had surveyed the

area of the fire from the Tower and had then gone on the river in a boat. He describes how he saw

> everybody endeavouring to remove their goods, and flinging into the river, or bringing them into lighters that lay off; poor people staying in their houses as long as till the very fire touched them, and then running into boats, or clambering from one pair of stairs by the waterside to another.

Pepys also noted that though the fire was raging in every direction no one was doing anything to stop it. This was the general mood at first. Every one was so taken by surprise by the rapid spreading of the fire that they could think of nothing but how to save themselves and as much of their property as they possibly could.

Responsibility for fighting the fire fell naturally upon the Lord Mayor, but, according to Pepys, the Lord Mayor at the time does not seem to have been a very forceful kind of person. He did try to organize the pulling down of houses, which was one of the customary ways of stopping a fire from spreading in London, but his men were overtaken by the fire before they could achieve their object. The difficulty of fighting such a fire once it had got a hold must have been enormous. There were no powerful pumps or hoses in those times, and, for some reason, the pipes bringing water from the New River dried up so that even this source of water was denied the fire-fighters. Finally, the Duke of York, the King's brother (who was afterwards to become James II), was put in command of the fire-fighting. He worked hard and capably, using gunpowder to blow up houses in the path of the fire, and thus cleared wide lanes over which the flames could not pass. After five days the fire was brought under control, but by this time over four-fifths of the City within the walls had been destroyed, and the area of smouldering ashes stretched from the Tower, in the east, to the Temple, in Fleet Street. St Paul's Cathedral was gone, as well as eighty-seven of the parish churches of the City, and all except a few of the halls of the

Great Companies, all the finest public buildings, and 13,000 houses. Moorfields was full of people who had lost their homes, camping among their possessions.

Yet, according to G. M. Trevelyan, it is unlikely that even half the population were left homeless. The bulk of the people now lived in the 'Liberties,' the suburbs without the walls, which had for the most part escaped the fire. He puts the population at this time at almost half a million. But within the City itself the transformation of dwelling-houses into offices and warehouses was already under way. This process has continued into our own times, and the number of people who actually live in the City is now only a few thousand, although hundreds of thousands come there each day to work. In the seventeenth century the nobles had already ceased to live in town-houses inside the City walls, and some wealthy merchants were following their example. Great numbers of the poorer sort were also living outside the walls.

THE REBUILDING OF THE CITY

Nevertheless, the majority of the merchants of London great and small lived as well as worked in the City, and it was these people that were hard hit by the Fire. It is difficult to imagine the loss in property and the damage to trade. Pepys notes in his diary that he met a Captain Cocke who put the value of the rents of the houses lost in the fire at £600,000 per year. Such a sum in present-day values of money would represent many millions of pounds. So we can imagine that every one in the City was anxious to rebuild as soon as possible. There were other reasons which made it important that London should get back to normal quickly. England was in the middle of a war against the Dutch. Every penny that London could earn by its trade was needed to help the war effort, and so were the heavy taxes which the country could draw from London.

No time was lost in getting down to the huge problem of the rebuilding of the burnt-out part. On September 10, only four days after the fire had stopped, Christopher Wren presented his plan for rebuilding to the King. On September 13 John Evelyn (whose diary is nearly as well known as that of Mr Pepys) sent in his plan. On September 20 and 21 two more were handed in. There may have been others of which we have no record. Yet none of these plans was adopted. Many have regretted that Wren's plan was never carried out, for it would have given London a magnificent centre, as splendid and spacious as that of any in the world. But the King rejected it within three days, and it seems now that he had some good reasons for doing so. It is hard to see where the money could have come from to carry out Wren's plan. All the old streets and buildings would have been swept away. We must remember that, although so many houses were burnt down, each man knew where his house had stood, and very likely he owned the ground it had stood on. To buy up all the land so that it could be parcelled out again according to the needs of Wren's plan would have called for a vast amount of money, and special powers to take over people's land whether they agreed or not. In the time of Charles II such sweeping measures would have hardly been possible. This whole question is discussed in detail in a book called *London, the Unique City*, by Steen Eiler Rasmussen, a Danish architect. In this fascinating book Rasmussen makes it clear that the King and his advisers early made up their minds that they should keep broadly to the principle that men should be allowed to rebuild their property on the site where the previous houses had stood, and that there should be no great changes in the general plan of the City. Nevertheless it was clear that certain directions regarding types of building material, the style of the houses themselves, the width of streets, and so forth would have to be issued. The King's first proclamation referred to all these matters and forbade any building until regulations had been issued, but it did assure the owners of property that they would have no cause to complain.

All the plans submitted to the King had been rejected because they were too sweeping in the changes that they recommended. Instead, the King appointed a committee (of which Wren was a member) which produced some sound and common-sense directions. They made provision that the size of houses, and particularly their height, should be controlled according to the width of the street they were built in. A narrow street could have only two-storey houses, while in wider streets they might be of three or four storeys. In the old London before the Fire tall houses had grown up in narrow streets, shutting out light and air, and making it easy for fires to spread. To make matters worse the houses had been built with the upper storeys jutting out towards each other, so that often the top storeys nearly touched. It was further directed that the new houses should be built of brick or stone, instead of in the half-timbered style which had been usual. Half-timber buildings had strong wooden beams, with the walls in between made of lath and plaster.

Of course the streets of the old City, which had grown up in medieval times, were too narrow. Advantage was taken of the rebuilding to widen the streets, but this was done in moderation. Streets which had no through traffic were allowed to remain fairly narrow. Main streets were widened considerably. This meant that certain people had to sell some of their ground to the City to make room for the wider roadways, but provision was made for the value of their ground to be fairly assessed.

Altogether the provisions of the committee which advised on the rebuilding of the City seem to have been wise and moderate and acceptable to most men. These provisions were passed into law by Parliament, and the citizens of London attacked the great task of rebuilding with such energy that, after four or five years only, the bulk of what had to be done was finished. A newer, healthier, and, indeed, a better-looking London had risen from the ruins. Many improvements were brought in as part of the general plan, such as better drainage for the streets and better sewers. Although the old haphazard street-plan of London was

kept, to the regret of many people at the time and for ever afterwards, Christopher Wren was given his chance to beautify the
City. The plans for the new St Paul's Cathedral and for forty-
nine City churches were his, and most of these beautiful buildings have survived for us to see to-day, even though Wren's
work suffered badly in the air attacks on London during the
Second World War. The rebuilding of St Paul's was paid for by
the whole of London by means of a tax on coal which Parliament
voted. (The illustration at page 65 shows Wren's original plan
for the rebuilding of the City.)

A New Style in London's New Buildings

There is one interesting fact about the rejected plans of Wren
and Evelyn and about the buildings of the new London which
now arose. The influence behind them was classical in origin,
whereas the old London had been Gothic in its general character.
These are terms used in architecture, and sometimes in the other
arts, to distinguish two great movements widely different in their
styles. They have their origin really in two different civilizations
in Europe. Gothic art and architecture was developed by the
Teutonic peoples of Northern Europe—that is, by the Germans,
the Flemish, the Dutch, the Frankish people of Northern France,
and by the English. Classical art and architecture inherited its
traditions from Greece and Rome, and found new expression
after the lapse of many centuries in Italy during the Renaissance,
of which we have already spoken.

The difference in style was seen, for example, in the new
churches and the new cathedral of St Paul's. Old St Paul's had
been a typical example of the 'pointed' Gothic style. It was a
tall building, with everything about it designed to increase the
effect of height. Tall, narrow windows with pointed arches, a
high arched roof to the nave and chancel, buttresses climbing up
in stages on the outside of the building, and in the centre a tall,

square tower, which had, before 1561, supported a tall spire. The new building, which Wren designed, had no towers or spires, no pointed arches or windows, no high, narrow transepts. Inside it was wide and spacious and light. Above the central part of the building rose a huge circular dome. Windows and pillars of Italian style were employed. The whole building was built of a white stone from Dorsetshire called Portland stone. When it was finished it bore more resemblance to St Peter's in Rome than to any cathedral yet built in England.

The flat-fronted dwelling-houses of brick copied their style for the most part from the Dutch architecture of the time. This was also classical in style, but relied for its effect on simple, good proportions, on graceful windows and doors, and on simpler decoration which could be carried out in brick without using expensive Portland stone. The latter was used for the most part in building churches or the houses of wealthy noblemen. About this time sash-windows came into use, very like the ones which we still have in many of our houses. The production of large clear panes of glass for windows, instead of the old dark 'bottle' glass, had also improved. It was thus possible to make the larger, well-proportioned type of window which these new houses demanded. Thus in the half-century or so after the Great Fire the face of London changed enormously. Except for the older streets, which still ran along the same course as before, the medieval city had almost disappeared. Wider streets, more spacious and graceful buildings in the classical style, made the City and West End of London worthy of the capital of England. Soon, indeed, London became the chief city of the whole island. for in 1707 England and Wales and Scotland became united under Queen Anne.

The foundations of the British Empire were now being laid. New colonies of British settlers were growing up in North America. The trade of the East India Company was growing fast. The British Navy was growing in power. The war with the Dutch came to an end, and the British and Dutch became

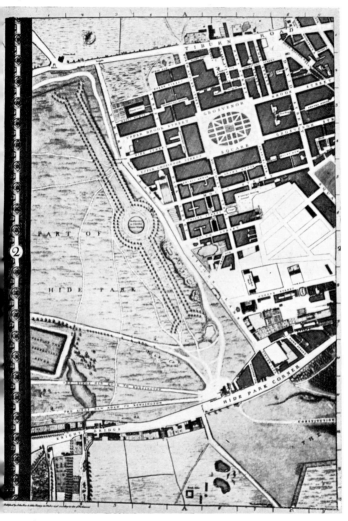

PART OF JOHN ROCQUE'S MAP OF LONDON IN 1746

Park Lane is called Tyburn Lane, and the Tyburn gallows can be
seen in the middle of the road in the top left-hand corner. The King's
Old Road and the King's New Road to Kensington run west from
Hyde Park Corner. The circular object in Hyde Park is the reservoir
of the Chelsea Water Works.

By courtesy of Associated Newspapers, Ltd

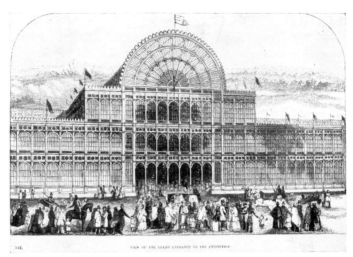

1851. THE CRYSTAL PALACE IN HYDE PARK

Revolutionary in design and materials, it expressed the confident spirit
of the Great Exhibition—the triumph of the Industrial Age.

1951. THE SOUTH BANK EXHIBITION

Focus of the Festival of Britain, its bold, exciting design matched the
spirit of a new era of rapid social and scientific change.

Festival of Britain copyright

allies against the ambitions of Louis XIV of France. Gradually Britain's naval power left behind that of her Dutch allies and of the French enemy. The British Navy began to rule the seas of the world and to give increasing security to the merchant ships that sailed them. As always, the biggest share of the increasing foreign trade fell to London.

LONDON RESUMES ITS EXPANSION

After the rebuilding of the burnt-out part of the old City London began to expand again. The old distinction between London and Westminster as separate towns was now a thing of the past. By the time of George I people when they spoke of London thought of the whole area which stretched from, say, Whitechapel almost to Hyde Park.

THE 'LIBERTIES' OUTSIDE THE WALLS

On the other side of the City a wide, built-up area stretched from Wapping, east of the Tower, northward through Whitechapel and Spitalfields as far as Shoreditch Church. Moorfields was still an open space, though much smaller than in former times, for houses had been built over part of it. It was to go on growing smaller and smaller until only upper Moorfields, which is now known as Finsbury Square, was left.

Northward beyond Cripplegate and Charterhouse, and far beyond the limits of the City Corporation's wards, the houses stretched out almost, but not quite, to Islington. Beyond Clerkenwell Green, which was still an old village green, the houses thinned out, until the Islington Road ran on through fields to the reservoir called the New River Head. Close by was a spring whose waters were said to have medicinal properties and to be like the waters of Tunbridge Wells. It was discovered by a

F

man called Sadler, who put up there a music room called Sadler's Wells Music House. For a time the place was actually called New Tunbridge Wells, but to-day we use the old name of Sadler's Wells, for the famous theatre which has now done so much to make ballet and opera popular in England stands on this very site to-day, and the spring still flows there.

This is how Islington seemed to Henri Misson, in the late seventeenth century:

> A large Village, half a League from London, where you drink Waters that do you neither Good nor Harm, provided you don't take too much of them. There is Gaming, Walking, Dancing; and a Man may spend an Hour there agreeably enough. It is not much flock'd to by People of Quality.

Most of this area east and north of the City proper, in the so-called 'Liberties' without the walls, was inhabited by the poorer craftsmen and unskilled labourers, who either went into the City each day for their work or were employed in small factories, furniture-makers, dye-works, weaving establishments in Spital-fields, and the like. The population of London was now so large that many small industries of various kinds were growing up in these parts to supply the wants of the citizens.

The 'West End' takes Shape

But the most important new building went on in the west. Here the 'West End' of London, which we still speak of to-day, was taking shape as a fashionable place in which to live. As early as the reign of Charles II Soho Square began to be developed in what were then open fields. Charles gave this land to his son the Duke of Monmouth, who built himself a town-house where now the Hospital for Women stands. Near-by Carlisle House was built for the first Earl of Carlisle. To the north, a few yards away, the Oxford Road ran west along the course of the present Oxford Street to Tyburn, where the Marble Arch now stands.

South of Soho, as far as Charing Cross, streets of fine new houses for fashionable people were built, and you may still see these houses in Soho to-day, many with plaques upon them to recall the famous people who have lived there. This remained a fashionable quarter until the early nineteenth century.

We have already mentioned how Covent Garden was laid out as a square in 1631. The architect of the whole design was Inigo Jones, one of the greatest of English architects, and the inspiration of his design was Italian. Covent Garden was (and still is, behind its market stalls) a piazza, the same in style and design as the great open spaces which grace the cities of Italy, and which are descended from the Forum which every city had in Roman times. The very name 'piazza' was actually given to the square in Covent Garden when it was first built, and one side of it was dominated by a church built in a severe classical style—the church of St Paul's, which still stands there. Thus the classical influence in architecture, and in this new way of building round a piazza or square, had already reached London before the Fire. Covent Garden was not the only square to be laid out in this way before the Fire, though it remained always the one which was most obviously Italian in style. Leicester Fields were transformed into Leicester Square about 1635. Bloomsbury Square was laid out in 1665 by the Earl of Southampton, after whom Southampton Row is named.

During the spread of new buildings to the west after the Fire the building of squares became an outstanding feature of the new London. We have seen how Soho Square began. By 1681 the square was laid out. St James's Square, much farther to the west, was laid out three years later. It is still one of the most beautiful of the London squares and contains many gracious houses, a good many of which date from the time of its creation. It has remained a fashionable place to live right up to the present day, though the number of private dwelling-houses is growing rapidly fewer, and soon, perhaps, none will be left.

Here is a rather delightful letter written by Isabella, Lady

Wentworth, who went house-hunting in the square about twenty years after it was built:

MY DEARIST AND BEST OF CHILDREN,

I have been to see a very good hous in St Jamsis Squair. It has thre large rooms forward and two little ons backward, closetts and marble chimney peicis, and harths to al the best rooms, and iron backs to the chimneys. Thear is twoe prety closets with chimneys and glas over them, and picturs in the wenscoat and top and slips of boards for the hangings. Thear will want little to be dun to it. Thear is back stairs, twoe coach housis, and stable for ii horses, rooms over for sarvents, very good offisis, a yard for the drying of cloaths, and leds for that purpus, a stable yard and a hors pond and back gate, which I forgot the street's name it goes into. Thear is a handsom roome al wenscaoted for the steward to dyne in, and another good roome for the other sarvents to dyne in even with the kitchin belowe stairs under the hall and parlors. It was my Lord Sunderland's, it was to little for them. They sold it to a marchant whoe sent his foolish neaphew whoe could not tell me the prise.

Near by King Charles II took great interest in the replanting and beautifying of St James's Park, which was carried out at his command. The Park was laid out on formal lines, according to the fashion of the times, and a great stretch of water was formed in the centre of it, which still remains one of the Park's great beauties.

All through the reigns of Charles II, William and Mary, and Queen Anne the houses marched westward, and the new streets and squares of graceful houses rose steadily. Names familiar to all who live in London (and to many who do not) begin to appear on maps—Piccadilly, Haymarket, Jermyn Street, Savile Row. Grosvenor Square was laid out in 1695, Berkeley Square in 1698. In 1705 Buckingham House was built at the west end of St James's Park for the Duke of Buckingham. Not until 1762 did it become a royal palace. In that year it was bought by King George III, but the front which we look at when we pass Buckingham Palace to-day was not added until 1847 and rebuilt in 1913.

Early Georgian London

By the time of George I the houses were reaching out to Park Lane, then known as Tyburn Lane, along the edge of Hyde Park. The area between Park Lane and Soho Square was still being developed. Hanover Square was being built in 1718, and soon afterwards the bricklayers and the stonemasons were busy north of Oxford Street in Cavendish Square, Chandos Street, Harley Street, and Welbeck Street.

The area bounded on the east and west by Regent Street and Park Lane, and on the north and south by Oxford Street and Piccadilly, is still spoken of to-day as Mayfair. The name has its origin in a fair which used to take place in the area now occupied by Curzon Street. It began in the days of Edward I and continued until after the year 1800, by which time it had acquired a very evil reputation. Sometimes it was called St James's Fair, but more often simply Mayfair.

From the bottom of Park Lane a royal road ran west through Hyde Park—the King's Road to Kensington Palace. In later times this became the King's Old Road, because George II built a new road some distance to the south of it. The old road became a favourite place for driving in carriages or riding horses, and in time it came to be the Rotten Row that we know to-day, with a specially prepared surface suitable for horses. But nobody knows whether it is called Rotten Row because of the material used on it, or because the name is a corruption of *Route du Roi*. (See illustration at page 80.)

Thus London began to shape itself into the broad divisions which are still familiar to us. To the east and north-east the home of the poor, working people; in the City itself the bankers and merchants; round Fleet Street and the Strand the colleges and chambers of the lawyers, the Temple, Lincoln's Inn, Clifford's Inn, and so on. In Westminster the House of Commons sat in St Stephen's Chapel and the Lords in the Court of Requests. In the streets round about were to be found the offices of various

Government departments. Finally came the West End, the abode of wealth and rank and fashion, pushing steadily farther westward, as we have seen. Perhaps this westward movement had something to do with the fact that after 1696 the old Palace of Whitehall was no more. Most of it disappeared in a disastrous fire and was never rebuilt. Only the Banqueting House, designed by Inigo Jones, now the home of the Royal United Service Institution, still survives to remind us of past glories—and past tragedies. It was from one of the windows of this building that Charles I stepped out on to the scaffold on a cold January morning of the year 1649, and bared his neck to the headman's axe. So, until King George III bought Buckingham House, the Court moved between St James's, Kensington Palace, and Hampton Court, encouraging by its presence in these parts the westerly movement of fashionable London.

South of the river, by the time of George I, Southwark had extended southward at least as far as the site of the Elephant and Castle and eastward through the rural surroundings of Bermondsey to Rotherhithe and beyond. To the west a fringe of buildings ran along Bankside, an area of doubtful reputation, towards Lambeth Marsh, formerly a desolate area, but now a pleasant place of market-gardens dotted with clusters of country dwellings here and there and well provided with tea-gardens where refreshment and light entertainment such as music and singing were provided. There were several large pleasure gardens, with long walks laid out with bowers and statuary, where meals of all sorts could be obtained and where ambitious displays of fireworks were staged. The most famous of these were Paris Garden, near Bankside, Cupers Garden (also called Cupid's Garden), close by the site of the Festival of Britain exhibition at the end of Waterloo Bridge, and—most famous of all—the great gardens at Vauxhall. These pleasure gardens were very popular—indeed, at times, almost too popular, as the following quotation from Horace Walpole's *Letters* shows:

May 11, 1769: I cannot say last night was very agreeable. There was what they called a *ridotto al fresco* at Vauxhall, for which one paid half-a-guinea, though, except some thousand more lamps and a covered passage all round the garden, which took off from the garden-hood, there was nothing better than on a common night. Mr Conway and I set out from his house at eight o'clock; the tide and torrent of coaches was so prodigious, that it was half-an-hour after nine before we got half way from Westminster Bridge. We then alighted; and after scrambling under bellies of horses, through wheels, and over posts and rails, we reached the gardens, where were already many thousand persons. Nothing diverted me but a man in a Turk's dress and two nymphs in masquerade without masks, who sailed amongst the company, and, which was surprising, seemed to surprise nobody. It had been given out that people were desired to come in fancied dresses without masks. We walked twice round and were rejoiced to come away, though with the same difficulties as at our entrance; for we found three strings of coaches all along the road, who did not move half a foot in half-an-hour. There is to be a rival mob in the same way at Ranelagh to-morrow; for the greater the folly and imposition the greater is the crowd. I have suspended the vestimenta that were torn off my back to the god of repentance, and shall stay away. Adieu!

As for the Port of London, it grew busier year by year, and below London Bridge, in the Pool of London, the masts of the crowded ships clustered like a forest. There were still very few docks for ships. For the most part goods were unloaded into lighters and ferried to the quayside and the small tidal basins on either side of the river. But the East India Company owned a small dock of some sort at Blackwall, and towards the end of the seventeenth century the Howland Great Wet Dock was started on the Surrey side, opposite the Isle of Dogs. This dock, later called the Greenland Dock, seems to have been the first true wet-dock built in London. It had space for over a hundred ships, which could remain afloat in it no matter what the state of the tide in the river. It formed the beginning of the great Surrey Commercial Dock system. At this time, in the first half of the eighteenth century, there were still few rivals to the position of the Port of London. Liverpool, Glasgow, Newcastle, and Hull were still comparatively unimportant places. Outside of London the most important towns were Bristol and Norwich. Although Bristol ranked next to London as a port, its sea-borne trade was only about a tenth of that of the capital.

London had a monopoly of the East India trade and still handled most of the trade with Europe, the Mediterranean, and Africa. In addition, London had big interests in much of the trade that went on inside England itself. All kinds of goods produced in the provinces were bought and sold in London, perhaps by men who never saw the actual goods themselves, but simply bought them from one owner and sold them to another, on paper.

Already London was beginning to show some of the unpleasant things which distinguished most of our big towns seventy or a hundred years later. There was much poverty and overcrowding among the skilled labourers and dockers; the living-quarters of these people were declining into horrible slums. London was growing too fast for the authorities to give proper attention to the good government of these poorer areas. From this time until far into the nineteenth century this problem was to remain, defeating the efforts of local authorities and private charity.

LONDON ON THE EVE OF THE INDUSTRIAL REVOLUTION

By the middle of the eighteenth century, then, London could look back on a hundred years of ceaseless growth since the disaster of the Great Fire. The ancient City of London still retained its independence within its old boundaries, and continued to increase in wealth and power, but it could no longer speak for the whole of London, which now contained perhaps 700,000 people and covered an area three or four times as large as that part governed by the City Corporation. London was now a place of world importance, the capital of a nation with a growing empire overseas and a great future opening out before her. London's new buildings, its wider streets, its spacious squares, its fashionable quarters with their air of quiet wealth and comfort, were the outward signs of the revolution in England's position which had begun over two hundred years before, and which was now bearing fruit. Sea-borne trade and sea-power were carrying England forward on a tide of fortune, and in this movement London was the leader.

A vivid picture of the rough, vigorous life of London at this time comes, as is so often the case, from a foreigner, Georg Lichtenberg, in his book *Visits to England*:

> All this appears like an enchantment to the unaccustomed eye; there is therefore all the more need for circumspection in viewing all discreetly; for scarcely do you stop than, crash! a porter runs you down by crying "By your leave," when you are lying on the ground. In the middle of the street roll chaises, carriages, and drays in an unending stream. Above this din and the hum and clatter of thousands of tongues and feet one hears the chimes from church towers, the bells of the postmen, the organs, fiddles, hurdy-gurdies, and tambourines of English mountebanks, and the cries of those who sell hot and cold viands in the open at the street corners. Then you will see a bonfire of shavings flaring up as high as the upper floors of the houses in a circle of merrily shouting beggar-boys, sailors, and rogues. Suddenly a man whose handerchief has been stolen will cry, "Stop thief," and every one will begin running and pushing and shoving—many of them not with any desire of catching the thief, but of prigging for themselves, perhaps, a watch or purse.

Look also at the lower illustration at p. 65.

To the Londoner of that day, rolling at a fair speed over the wider, better-paved streets in one of the coaches which were now so fashionable and so numerous, it must have seemed that London was at the peak of its prosperity and that a few more years would see the limit of its growth. But already there were new forces at work, as yet but dimly felt, which were to change the face of England itself, and to alter London so much that this great capital city of the mid-eighteenth century would be swallowed up in a sea of buildings stretching out for miles round it. The very roads over which these London coaches of the eighteenth century rolled had a decisive part to play in these great changes, for without the improved roads which were then being built the Industrial Revolution, which was just beginning, could hardly have got under way.

In the England of the seventeenth and early eighteenth centuries the roads were actually, for the most part, in a worse condition than they had been at the time of the Roman occupation. But the increasing use of coaches instead of horses for travelling led to a demand for roads usable in all weathers, and a steady improvement began as the system of granting powers to private companies to maintain stretches of roadway and to charge a toll to those using them came more and more into use. So, thanks to these turnpike companies, as they were called, road travel grew ever easier and swifter. As we have seen in an earlier chapter, the main roads of England, established by the Romans, converged on London. Thus London was bound to feel very quickly the effects of the new industrial and agricultural changes which were now at work and which we shall examine in the next chapter.

Chapter Six

LONDON AND THE INDUSTRIAL REVOLUTION

THE story of the great movement called the Industrial Revolution occupies an important place in the history of England and, indeed, in the history of the world, for it is the story of one of those periods which, like the rise and fall of the Roman Empire or like the twin movements of the Renaissance and the Reformation, have had great consequences for the whole of mankind.

As is usually the case with such great changes, it is difficult to say when the Industrial Revolution first began, and it is also difficult to say which were the most important influences within this great movement. For there was not one single event or invention which brought it about. There were rather a chain of circumstances which all worked together to encourage the growth of new ways of producing both food and goods. These new methods of production changed first the life of the farm labourer and then the life of the small craftsman and industrial worker, leading to the collection of many people in new towns round the new factories which were built.

CHANGES IN THE COUNTRYSIDE

We have seen the way in which London developed during the early part of the eighteenth century. Equally great changes came to the English countryside; but before these changes came about the English town or village lived its own self-contained life, remote from its neighbours and to a large extent self-supporting. For a large part of the year it was cut off from the outside world because of the poor roads, which became impassable to anything but horse-traffic in bad weather. The village or small town had its own wheelwrights, carpenters, blacksmiths, and shoemakers; it supplied practically all its own food. The only things it needed to bring in from outside were comparative luxuries. Even the spinning of wool and the making of cloth, which had been a source of wealth in England for so many centuries, were still largely carried on in people's own homes, in their villages. Indeed, most manufacture was carried on in the villages because the methods used were simple and did not need large machines.

NEW FARMING METHODS: THE ENCLOSURES

Outside the villages and towns were the fields, still cultivated in many cases on the old open-field system, which had survived from the Middle Ages. One man might own strips of land in each of three different fields. In one field wheat was grown, the second field lay fallow, and cattle were allowed to graze on it, the third field grew oats or barley. These fields were very big and were owned in common by the village. They were common land. This ownership of his own particular strips of land gave a man independence, but it was difficult to carry out any improvements to such land, because so many people were concerned if any change was to be made.

In the eighteenth century great progress began to be made in the manuring of the field, in methods of sowing, in the improvement of land by draining and by introducing new crops, and in the breeding of cattle. These methods could be properly used only on small, compact fields surrounded by hedges. Thus the great landowners, who were anxious to bring in these new methods of increasing the fertility of the soil, began to enclose waste land in order to cultivate it, and also they began to enclose the common land, either by agreement with the villagers concerned or by purchase. On the whole those who enclosed the land and improved it meant well. Such men as Coke of Norfolk, a famous landowner who was a leader in the new methods of agriculture, were sincere in their aim to benefit not only themselves, but their tenants. But there were others, of course, whose aim was only to enrich themselves and to obtain land as cheaply and quickly as possible. Enclosure Acts were rushed through Parliament at each session. By 1837 almost all the open corn-land had been enclosed.

The results of this Agricultural, or Agrarian, Revolution were undoubtedly of great benefit to the country as a whole. Much more corn was raised and many more animals. It also became possible to raise enough feeding-stuffs to keep a good many animals alive throughout the winter. Until this time it had been the custom always to slaughter most of the livestock in the autumn and to salt the meat for eating during the winter. But in the later eighteenth century it became possible to have fresh meat all the year round. This increase in food-stuffs was most valuable to Great Britain, for the population was now beginning to increase quite rapidly. It is not easy to assign a definite reason for this increase. Better medical knowledge may have been one of the causes.

But the enclosure of land had evil results as well. Many men who had been small independent farmers, even though poor, were now dispossessed. Instead of their land they had a few guineas, which were soon spent. Most of them went to work on the great estates for a weekly wage. But many could not or would not do this, and they began to drift towards the towns.

THE TURNPIKE ROADS

Here we see how many different circumstances can combine to bring about a single great effect. The new trunk-roads, which were also a notable feature of the eighteenth century in England, made it possible for these landless farm labourers to move about the country far more easily than they could have done at any earlier time. The same roads (and the canals, which were built at the same time) also encouraged the movement of industry from the villages into the larger towns, where factories began to be built.

TYBURN TURNPIKE
After Rowlandson

The second half of the eighteenth century saw a swift extension of the system of improving roads by private enterprise both at home and on the continent of Europe, and consequently a great increase in travel. The companies which built the new roads were called turnpike companies. They obtained power from Parliament to charge a toll to all those using a certain stretch of road, and in return they undertook to be responsible for its up-keep. The gates which they set across the road to stop travellers so that the toll could be collected were called 'turnpikes.' These companies were energetic and keen to find better methods of constructing and surfacing roads. The finest of the turnpike roads were built by John MacAdam, whose name is still used for the type of road surface which he perfected. On these roads coaches were able to travel at up to ten miles an hour, but this speed was not reached until the early nineteenth century, when coach-building was also much improved.

The Canals

At the same time as the turnpike roads were being built the Duke of Bridgewater led the way in the construction of artificial waterways, or canals. His first project was to cut a canal from Worsley to Manchester so that coal could be carried from his collieries to the ships. That was in 1759, and during the next half-century the canal movement spread steadily until England was covered with the waterways which we still possess to-day. Until the coming of the railways they were enormously popular for they were easily the cheapest and most effective way that had yet been found of moving coal and heavy goods through the country.

These new roads and canals stimulated trade enormously, for they made it possible for people and goods to move about with much greater ease. Manufactured goods from the interior of England began to find their way in much greater quantity to the ports to be sent abroad, and goods imported by sea could now be sold in the interior of England much more cheaply because of lower costs of transport.

Mechanical Inventions

Still more influences were operating at the same time to increase the production of goods in Britain. The age of invention was beginning. The inventions which had the most immediate and marked effect were in spinning and weaving. In 1733 John

Kay invented a 'flying' shuttle, which could be sent mechanically from one side of the loom to the other instead of being thrown by hand. About thirty years later Hargreaves invented the spinning jenny, a device which could turn a number of spindles at the same time. Soon afterwards Arkwright invented a way of using water-power to turn spindles. Finally, Crompton's 'mule' combined the application of power to the driving of a number of spindles. Before long these machines made it possible for a few people to supervise the spinning of wool or cotton, and especially cotton, on scores or even hundreds of spindles at the same time. In 1769 James Watt had produced his first steam-engine, and in 1785 the first steam-engine designed to drive machinery was installed in a cotton-mill in Nottingham. A few years later an improved type of weaving-loom was invented which could be driven by water-power or, later, by steam-power. Thus the arts of spinning and weaving were altered out of all recognition, and so were the lives of those who worked in these industries. No longer were they occupations which could be carried on in the villages and the home. The new machines were large, heavy, and expensive. They had to be housed in factories in the towns, where people from surrounding villages came to work. Henceforth the worker had to come to the machine. There was no shortage of labour, for, as we have seen, there were plenty of landless farm-workers ready to try their luck in the towns.

The cotton industry was particularly affected by the new developments, and a great expansion took place, particularly in Lancashire. New towns began to grow up with great speed, and, though jobs were plentiful, living and housing conditions were poor. Other types of manufacture also began to develop, and the factory system became widespread. In all these industries iron was needed, and the production of iron began to expand rapidly. It was enabled to do so because of progress in the use of coal and coke to smelt iron, in place of charcoal. Other technical inventions in iron-working followed, and great ironworks arose where coal and iron were found lying close together.

Thus the foundations of the modern industrial society were laid, and the Napoleonic wars, which came at the end of the eighteenth century, gave fresh encouragement to the swift progress of the new methods of production.

London finds the Money for New Enterprises

All this new development, in improved farming methods, in the enclosure of land (which was immensely costly), in better stock-breeding, in the building of canals and roads, and in the building of factories and machines, needed money. What people now call the capitalist system was then coming into being at a great rate. Instead of a country of small businesses and small farms, mostly worked by the people who owned them, Britain was changing into a country where there were many large estates or large firms, each owned by one person or by a small group. The employer supplied the money and the machines. Those employed had, as a rule, no share in the ownership of the enterprise, and were dependent on their employment, which was often very uncertain, for the means to live. Many people regret that this way of operating business and agriculture developed, for it brought fierce competition and insecurity to a great number of people. Others will say, and with truth, that these developments brought rapid progress and a great increase in the production of every kind of goods. In any event, this was the course that affairs did take, and large amounts of money were needed for investment of all kinds. London played a great part in the supplying of this money and so shared in the beginnings of Britain's industrial expansion.

New Docks for London's Growing Trade

It is hard to exaggerate the way in which London dominated the trade of Britain during these busy times—between, say, 1750 and 1820—both within the country and overseas. It was during

G

this time that the Port of London became specially concerned with a type of trade known as 'entrepot' trade, which still continues to be one of the most important activities. Not only did London import vast quantities of goods and raw materials which were sent out to other parts of England, it also brought in from all parts of the British Isles and from all parts of the world goods of all kinds which were stored in its warehouses, and then sent

SHIPYARD AT DEPTFORD
After Rowlandson

off again in other ships to fresh buyers all over Europe and in many other countries. Thus a large part of the goods coming into London Docks were not used in Britain at all. They were cargoes in which London's money had been invested in order to be sold at a profit to a foreign customer. The shipping trade continued to grow all through this period, and by the end of the eighteenth century new docks were urgently needed. The West India and London Docks were started about this time, and were both completed in 1805. In the following year the new East India Docks were opened. Thus, in the middle of the great struggle against Napoleon, London's trade continued to expand. In the very year of final victory against Napoleon, in 1815, the Surrey Commercial Docks, which are on the south side of the river, were opened.

THE GROWTH OF LONDON FROM 1750 TO 1820

Traffic grew heavier in the greater London which now stretched out round the old City area. More and more coaches rolled through its streets, and as the turnpike roads throughout England improved with each year more and more long-distance coaches reached London. The barrier of the river Thames now began to prove a great hindrance to traffic, for there was still only the one bridge, old London Bridge, by which to cross the river. About 1756 it was cleared of all the houses which had been built upon it, so that it was less of a hindrance to traffic, but even before this new bridges across the Thames had been begun. Westminster Bridge was opened in 1750, and Blackfriars Bridge in 1770. These new bridges led to the construction of new roads across St George's Fields, in Lambeth, and hastened the development of this part of London. Although Lambeth Marsh retained its open fields for many a year, the houses began to spread out through South Lambeth towards Kennington, and from the village of Newington Butts eastward towards Kent Street, which we now call the Old Kent Road. (Incidentally, this road, which leads on to the Dover Road, follows the line of the southern part of Watling Street, which ran from Dover through London as far as Chester.) Southward from Newington Butts the houses ran along the Walworth Road towards the village of Camberwell.

All round London the story was being repeated. London was creeping out, advancing slowly and steadily like the tide on the seashore, swallowing up the villages on its outskirts. Not that the villages themselves had remained unaltered. They too were expanding, sharing in the prosperity of London, which bought up all their market-garden and dairy produce, found jobs for many of their inhabitants, and provided many rich residents who

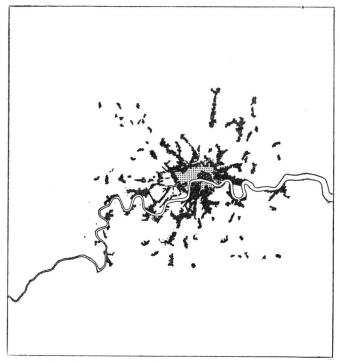

THE DISTRIBUTION OF LONDON'S POPULATION IN 1820

KEY

White dots on black: Area of City of London.

Black dots on white: Limits reached by 1750-60.

Black: Subsequent expansion to 1820, with marked growth of villages round London.

found it pleasant to have a house in the country, yet not too far from London Town, where their business lay. Chelsea and Kensington had long ago become fashionable places for well-to-do Londoners to live. Battersea, Wandsworth, Putney, Fulham, and Hammersmith were no longer tiny hamlets but were growing up into large villages. So were Streatham, Dulwich, Sydenham, and Lewisham, in the south. On the east Deptford and Greenwich were places of considerable size, already almost linked together by their own growth.

Horace Walpole, writing in 1791, had a prophetic vision of the future:

> The Duke of St Albans has cut down all the brave old trees at Hanworth, and consequently reduced his park to what it issued from —Hounslow-heath; nay, he has hired a meadow next to mine, for the benefit of embarkation; and there lie all the good old corpses of oaks, ashes, and chestnuts, directly before *your* windows, and blocking up one of my views of the river! but so impetuous is the rage for building, that his Grace's timber will, I trust, not annoy us long. There will soon be one street from London . . . to every village ten miles round! Lord Camden has just let ground at Kentish Town for building fourteen hundred houses—nor do I wonder; London is, I am certain, much fuller than ever I saw it. I have twice this spring been going to stop my coach in Piccadilly, to inquire what was the matter, thinking there was a mob—not at all; it was only passengers.

By 1820 or so houses had spread along the south bank of the river, linking Deptford and Greenwich with Bermondsey and Southwark. North of the river the creation of London squares and planned estates continued. In the area north of New Oxford Street, which we now call Bloomsbury, the Duke of Bedford began to lay out an estate of more than a hundred acres. Bedford Square itself was built by about 1780. Farther west the splendid thoroughfare, Portland Place, was built, and farther west still another fashionable new estate stretched northward as far as the New Road from Paddington to Islington. The little village of St Mary-le-bone was engulfed in this last expansion, but did not entirely disappear. To this day Marylebone High Street has something of the air of a small-town shopping-centre, though the buses roar past the great stores in Oxford Street, just a few minutes away. It has remained separate, the centre of its own district. The High Street itself follows the line it took long ago when its houses stood upon the banks of the Tyburn Brook.

The New Road when it was first built was looked upon as a notable improvement to London's communications. It connected the large village or small town of Paddington with the other large village of Islington, and at first it ran for most of its length through open fields. From Islington the City Road ran, as it still does, into the City of London as far as Finsbury Square. Thus the New Road provided a convenient way of entering or leaving the City without having to go through the crowded streets of the Strand, Holborn, and the West End. It was thought that this would do much to relieve London's traffic problem. Indeed, it did, and this road is still an important one, carrying much traffic. The western half of it, running from the Edgware Road to Camden Town, is now the Marylebone Road. But before long the houses were spreading across the New Road into Somers Town and Pentonville and Camden Town.

Farther to the north-west lay the high ground of Hampstead and Highgate. These also were old-established villages which had long ago begun to grow owing to the building of houses for well-to-do people who had to be near London, but did not wish to live in it. By 1820 houses had spread along the main roads linking these places with London. The same thing had happened to the north of Islington, where houses ran along the main road to Holloway. This habit of building houses along a busy road from one suburb or town to another is sometimes called 'ribbon' development. It has been a marked feature in the growth of London right up to very recent times.

In the north-east great development had taken place by 1820 in Hackney, Bethnal Green, Stepney, and Poplar. Farther out the villages of Stoke Newington, Lower Clapton, Old Ford, and Stratford-le-Bow had grown much larger. For many young men, and women too, in these villages and in the towns and villages for a hundred miles round, London was the great magnet which drew them towards it. It was a fabulous place, full of great people, and of strange sights, and full of opportunity, or so it seemed. And, with the increased speed of coaches over the good roads, a young man a hundred miles from London might reach it in a day's journey for a sum of ten shillings. A hundred years or so earlier the same journey might have taken four or five days.

London nears the Limit of the Gravel Terraces

The expansion of London had now reached a rather interesting stage. In Chapter I we mentioned the gravels which are scattered at various points in the Thames Valley on top of the London clay. The buildings of London had now pushed out so far that in some directions, particularly in the north-west, they had practically reached the limits of the gravel terraces on which London had grown up. The villages round London had also, for the most part, grown up where patches of gravel offered suitable ground for human dwellings and springs of water for drinking purposes.

Regent Street and Regent's Park

It is impossible to describe in detail all the improvements and fine new buildings that were added to London during the period from 1750 to 1820, but we cannot omit to mention the important town-planning schemes successfully carried through by the Prince Regent, afterwards King George IV. Much is said in history books about the faults of this extravagant prince, but, at all events, he gave his name to an age, to a style of living, and to a type of architecture. The word 'Regency' may stand for a period when royalty was brought into disrepute by scandal and loose living, but it stands also for a period when both art and architecture were encouraged. The Prince Regent had grand ideas about the style of living suited to his position as uncrowned King of England. He lived at Carlton House, which lay where the Duke of York's Column now stands, at the foot of Waterloo Place, and his favourite architect, John Nash, had already made some improvements to this palace. But Nash was also employed on the laying-out of Regent's Park, which was then going on according to his designs. This was Crown land, and the Prince planned to have a new house in the new park, where he should be able to enjoy country air while still near enough to London to attend to State affairs.

But the area between Carlton House and Regent's Park was for the most part a district of narrow streets crowded with poorer people, though here and there were some fine squares. This area certainly offered no 'royal road' for the Prince to use on his journeys between country and town. So the Prince decided to build one. To John Nash fell the great task of planning the new road and the least expensive way of building it. To the Prince went the labour of obtaining Parliamentary approval and a grant of money to undertake the work. Even with due regard for economy, the amount of demolition necessary was still very great. Entire streets were pulled down. The street had to be curved in places to avoid property which was too expensive to be destroyed. But finally Regent Street stretched from Carlton House up Lower Regent Street to where Piccadilly Circus now spreads out. Then it swept round to the left in a quadrant of a circle. This 'Quadrant,' which was the name actually given to this part of the street, was lined on both sides with pillared arcades covering the pavements. They may be seen in pictures of old Regent Street. None of them or of the old buildings themselves now remain, but the curve of the street has been preserved. The eye was carried round the curve by the continuous frontage of the houses, and the whole effect was thought to be most elegant. Indeed, this Regent Street was said by some to be the finest street in Europe. It continued northward to where the B.B.C. building now stands. From here the approach to Regent's Park was completed by the splendid Portland Place, which was already in existence, having been designed and built by the Adam brothers in association with the Duke of Portland, who owned the land.

Thus the Prince's splendid street was built, and Regent's Park laid out and generously made available by the Crown for the enjoyment of the general public. Round the Park Nash built the huge blocks of houses embellished with pillars and porticoes and groups of classical statuary with names like Cumberland Terrace, Hanover Terrace, Sussex Place, which recall the members of the House of Hanover at that time. The Regent's Canal was constructed as part of the whole gigantic scheme. It passed through the Park on its way from the docks and the East End to its junction with the Grand Union Canal, in the West of London, and its waters were used to form an ornamental lake.

But the whole original purpose of the scheme was never carried out. The Prince Regent became King George IV and began to alter and add to Buckingham Palace. Carlton House was pulled down, and the busy Nash built Carlton House Terrace in its place, as noble a street as any in London. So, though George IV's country-house in Regent's Park never came to be built, and though Nash's Regent Street frontage has been replaced by heavier and clumsier buildings, London must be thankful for the desire of the First Gentleman in Europe to enhance his own dignity by giving London a grander appearance. It has given London a fine thoroughfare sweeping through the West End; it has given her the broad expanse of Regent's Park surrounded by terraces which remind us of an age when her accumulated wealth began to be spent on the pursuit of elegance in architecture, in fashion, and in modes of living.

London was now the rich capital of a growing empire. It was now one of the largest cities in the world. As already mentioned, its population in the first half of the eighteenth century was

700,000 or more. By 1820 the number of people in Greater London was more than one and a quarter million. Two causes contributed to this great increase in numbers. First, there was, as we have seen, an unending stream of newcomers from the country come to seek their fortune. Secondly, and much more surprising, there was, despite the fearsome slums which disfigured many parts of London, a steady decrease in the death-rate in London. By 1820 it had fallen to one in forty. In this respect London shared with the rest of the country the benefits of a considerable advance in medical knowledge and skill.

In medicine, as in so much else, the Age of Progress was dawning; the wonderful nineteenth century, in which so many new inventions were to be born, was already giving a foretaste of the splendid things to come. As early as 1821 a cross-Channel steamboat went into service between England and France. In the same year Michael Faraday, in the laboratories of the Royal Institution, was already engaged on experiments in electro-magnetism which were to end in harnessing a mighty new power to the service of man. In a few years more John Dalton was to be honoured by the Royal Society for his development of the Atomic Theory, without which the staggering progress of modern physics could hardly have begun.

But the working out of all these wonders lay still in the future. In the next half-century the steady increase in engineering and mechanical skill, the steady application of steam-power to ever-new types of machinery, the steady improvement in fast transport, and the steady increase in wealth and population were to make London expand at such a rate that Georgian London was ringed round with mile upon mile of new suburbs, until the mass of streets and houses reached a size the like of which the world had never known.

Chapter Seven

THE GREAT EXPANSION

O UR story of London's growth has brought us near to our own times. Only a little over a hundred years separates us from that London of the early nineteenth century which we have just described. That London could look back on 1800 years of history, yet the changes that were to come in a single century were to be greater than all that had happened in the many centuries that were past. But the story is not altogether one of splendid progress. Up to the middle of the nineteenth century, at least, there is a dark tale of human misery, poverty, and unemployment to set beside the figures of increasing trade, increasing wealth, and increasing population.

THE DIVISIONS OF LONDON ABOUT 1837

The increase in London's trade was certainly impressive. Between 1819 and 1859 the trade of the Port of London increased by 200 per cent.—that is, it trebled itself. But London was no longer dependent merely on the Port of London for its business activities. Sir Laurence Gomme, who became Clerk to the London County Council in 1900, described the London of 1837 as consisting of these divisions: the City, the centre of trade and commerce; Spitalfields, chiefly silk manufacture; Whitechapel, sugar-refining; Southwark (along the Thames bank as far as Vauxhall), industries such as dye-works, tanneries, glass-works, iron-foundries, boot and shoe factories, breweries; in the west (from Temple Bar to Knightsbridge), the Court, Parliament and the Government offices, the Inns of Court, and the Law Courts, some very fashionable shopping-quarters; in the north-west, the most fashionable dwelling-houses in the new streets and squares; in the north (including Pentonville and Somers Town), the middle class. In all parts of London there were, of course, large numbers of small tradesmen and small craftsmen of various sorts. London was so large a market for so many different kinds of things that many people inside London were concerned solely with making the clothes, shoes, furniture, and so on that its citizens used or in bringing in and selling the food that they needed. Almost anyone, of whatever trade or of none at all, might hope to find a living in London. So the population continued to increase, as more and more people came there. Unemployment, however, was beginning to show, as Charles Greville, the famous Regency diarist, makes clear:

A man came yesterday from Bethnal Green with an account of that district. There are all weavers, forming a sort of separate community; there they are born, there they live and labour, and there they die. They neither migrate nor change their occupation; they can do nothing else. They have increased in a ratio at variance with any principles of population, having nearly tripled in twenty years, from 22,000 to 62,000. They are for the most part out of employment, and can get none. 1100 are crammed into the poor house, five or six in a bed; 6000 receive parochial relief. The parish is in debt; every day adds to the numbers of paupers, and diminishes that of ratepayers. These are principally small shopkeepers, who are beggared by the rates. The district is in a complete state of insolvency and hopeless poverty, yet they multiply, and while the people look squalid and dejected, as if borne down by their wretchedness and destitution, the children thrive and are healthy. Government is ready to interpose with assistance, but what can Government do? We asked the man who came what could be done for them. He said "employment," and employment is impossible.

The Expansion of London up to 1860

By 1851 the population had increased to about 2,200,000, and by 1861 to about 2,800,000. Between 1801 and 1851 the population of Paddington soared from 2000 to 46,000. By 1861 a solid mass of new houses stretched from Paddington, in the west, to Old Ford and Stratford, in the east, on the fringe of the Lea Valley. Huge areas of new houses stretched out through Camden Town and Kentish Town, and lapped round the pleasant village of Hampstead. These new suburbs were linked with others north of Islington, covering Holloway and Upper Holloway as far as Highgate. East of these areas came Hackney, Stoke Newington, and Clapton, all of which were built up during this period.

On the south side of the river the same thing was happening. The population of South London increased by 400,000 between 1801 and 1851. In the great triangle bounded by Battersea, on the west, Greenwich, on the east, and Croydon, on the south, the houses spread out in all directions, linking old Southwark and Bermondsey with Camberwell, Lewisham, Penge, and Croydon. To the west of this chain of townships more building took place round old-established centres in Brixton, Stockwell, Kennington, and Clapham, and joined up with other new streets pushing out from the riverside parishes of Lambeth and Battersea. East of Camberwell other new areas pushed out through Peckham towards Deptford.

Thus, on both sides of the Thames, although certain great open spaces were preserved, enormous areas of ground were covered with street after street of houses stretching out in all directions. An interesting point about this expansion of London in the first half of the nineteenth century is that in some areas, particularly to the north-west, it went beyond the gravels on which practically the whole of the earlier London had grown up. London's growth was no longer influenced by such considerations as the nature of the land. Water could be pumped by large steam-

engines over considerable distances, so local water-supplies were
no longer an urgent problem. Gas began to be supplied to houses
for lighting after 1807. Such advances made easier the rapid
growth of new suburbs.

IMPROVEMENTS IN COMMUNICATION

But the most important influence in the growth of London in
the nineteenth century was the improvement in transport and
communications. Most of the spreading-out of the suburbs which
we have just described took place along the main roads. When
the most desirable building-plots along these roads were filled
the builders developed further streets in the areas behind them.
Those who could afford to live at a distance from the business
quarters of the great metropolis moved into these new areas,
leaving the crowded central districts to be packed more and
more tightly with those who could afford to live nowhere else.
This expansion and shifting of population could not have
happened without improved roads, better and faster carriages,
and better public transport. The roar and clatter of London's
traffic in the early days of Queen Victoria's reign must have been
not unlike that of the London streets to-day. The streets were
full of vehicles spinning along at a good pace with the clip-clop
of horses' hooves and the rattle of iron-shod wheels. Fast mail-
coaches ran out of London on all the main roads to all parts of
England. Six hundred stage-coaches ran local services between
London and towns up to twenty miles out. Within London
itself omnibuses were coming into use. The first one to be seen
on the London streets was owned by a man called Shillibeer,
who had seen omnibuses in use in Paris. Shillibeer's omnibus
ran from Paddington Green to the Bank of England—that is,
from the heart of one of the new well-to-do suburbs to the heart
of the business quarter. Of course, these small horse-buses (the
first one carried eighteen passengers) became very popular, and

when the London General Omnibus Company was formed in the middle of the century it bought up several hundred which were by that time running in various parts of London.

Thomas Carlyle thought of the bustling life of the streets as a stream of living letters:

July 6, 1834. The London streets themselves are a quite peculiar object, and I daresay of almost *inexhaustible* significance. There is such a torrent of vehicles and faces: the slow rolling, all-defying wagon, like a mountain in motion, the dejected Hackney-coach, that "has seen better days," but goes along as with a tough uncomplaining patience, the gay equipage with its light bounding air, and *flunkies* of colour hanging behind it; the *distracted* Cab (a thing like a Cradle set aslant on its foot-end, where you sit open in front but free from rain), which always some *blackguard* drives, with the fury of Jehu; the huge Omnibus (a painted *Corn-kist*, of twenty feet long, set on four wheels: no, it cannot be *twenty* feet!) which runs along all streets from all points of the compass, as a sixpenny or shilling stage-coach towards 'The Bank' (of England); Butchers' and Brewers' and Bakers' Drays: all these, with wheelbarrows, trucks (hurlies) dogcarts, and a nameless flood of other *sma' trash*, hold on unweariedly their ever-vexed chaotic way. And then of foot-passengers! From the King to the Beggar; all in haste, all with a look of care and endeavour; and as if there *were* really "Deevil a thing but one man oppressing another." To wander along and read all this: it is reading one of the strangest everlasting *Newspaper Columns* the eye ever opened on. A Newspaper Column of *living* Letters (as I often say) that was printed in Eternity, and is here published only for a little while in TIME, and will soon be recalled and taken out of circulation again!

Before long the coaches and omnibuses began to have competition from a new form of transport which, eventually, was to sweep the coaches from the roads of England altogether. The railways came to London. The first line was from London to Greenwich; it was opened in 1836. In the next ten or fifteen years London shared to the full in the great rush to build railways, which went on at this time all over England. By 1850 all the new main-line railway companies had lines with a terminus in London. Thus the railways of England came to converge on London, just as the roads had done. These main-line termini were built as close as possible to the densely built-up area of

THE DISTRIBUTION OF LONDON'S POPULATION IN 1870

By this time the villages near London were completely linked up with the built-up central area, and there was great development in South London.

KEY

Black dots on white: Area of City of London.

London itself. Thus their positions on the map give a rough idea of the fringes of London between 1840 and 1850. But in some cases the railway terminus was pushed right inside the built-up area. Waterloo Station, for instance, which was built in 1848, occupied a site of this kind. Within ten or twenty years the new houses of London, pushing outward, had crept past the main railway stations. The great embankments, viaducts, and railway cuttings have cut up whole districts of London into uncomfortable patterns, making them ugly and sordid. But when they first came these main-line stations brought in more people and more goods, and added fresh vigour to the growth of London.

The map shows the extent of the built-up area in about the year 1870.

After about 1846 it was recommended that no new railways should be made above ground in the districts of central London. Already at this date people were looking forward to the time when the railways would have to go underground. And, indeed, it was not long before they began to do so. The earliest Metropolitan Railway began to operate in 1863. It had taken several years to build, and it ran under the New Road, from Farringdon Street, via King's Cross, Gower Street, Portland Road, Baker Street, and Edgware Road, to Bishop's Road, Paddington. Of course, this was not a true underground railway in the sense that London came to know the word later. It ran through a series of deep cuttings linked by short tunnels, and the trains were hauled by steam-engines. This made the tunnels very smoky and dirty. But it is a tribute to the immense progress that the nineteenth century was making in engineering skill that such a difficult undertaking could have been carried through successfully.

Social Troubles caused by Rapid Growth

It is not surprising that the speed of these huge changes in London during the first half of the nineteenth century should have produced many social problems. As has already been said, the new suburbs which were being built so rapidly to the north

H

and north-west of London were very largely for those who were tolerably well off. Many streets of the houses in which these people lived are still standing to-day in Camden Town, Kentish Town, and Holloway. Many are large, imposing houses, rather down at heel now, and split up into flats or bed-sitting-rooms, but all at one time were inhabited by a single family with perhaps two or even three servants. Others, smaller, needed only one servant. There are many other streets, too, of more modest houses, where servants—cheap as servants were in those days— were not provided for, but even these smaller houses were intended to house only solid citizens with a safe, secure way of life.

Such dwellings were far beyond the reach of the poorer citizens of London, who continued to crowd into the slum quarters of Central and East End districts. Many of them lived in conditions of incredible poverty and squalor. Every one has heard of the 'Hungry Forties,' those years when low wages and high prices for bread, caused by the Corn Laws, combined to bring hardship to working-class people all over England. Rich, prosperous London was not exempt from these effects. There was, indeed, in London, as elsewhere in Britain, a deep gulf between the upper and middle classes, on the one hand, and the working class, on the other. There were, one might say, two nations in Britain, and no one who had no direct contact with the poor had any conception of the conditions in which they lived. Men and women (and children too) worked long hours in bad conditions for a few shillings. In London one of the worst industries for poor wages was the cheap-clothing trade. Thousands of women worked eighteen hours a day, sewing shirts for twopence-halfpenny each or trousers for sevenpence a pair. Many families lived in one room, with hardly any furniture, a broken board for a table and a piece of plank laid across bricks for a seat. In the worst slums of London conditions were even worse than this. In the overcrowded quarters of the East End, in Southwark, in parts of Westminster, in Soho, and in St Giles (in the quarter which was cleared when New Oxford Street was built) were networks of courts and alleys which went by the nickname of 'rookeries' because so many people were packed into them. Henry Mayhew, one of the first of the enlightened journalists who began to tell people what conditions were like among the poor of London, found that in one court of thirty houses over nine hundred people were living!

THE LIFE OF LONDON'S POOR

Mayhew investigated the life of the working class and the poor of London for over twenty years, and in 1851 produced a great work, *London Labour and the London Poor*, which is a mine of information about these people. So strange are the tales he tells and the conditions he describes that sometimes one might think that he is describing some strange race of half-savage people rather than Londoners of the middle of the nineteenth century.

Complete ignorance prevailed among these people about anything outside their own daily struggle to make a living. The vast majority could not read or write and even if the parents could manage to keep a child from work in order to send him to school there were very few schools for the children of the poor. Most of these people had no religion or had lost what little they once had. Many had never heard of Jesus Christ; others confused Him with Adam or Moses. Clergymen were 'udged solely by the amount of attention they devoted to the sick and the poor—and unfortunately, at this time, many of them were lacking in their devotion to such work of Christian charity. Drunkenness was very prevalent among the poor. Cheap gin, a potent, dangerous spirit, with all kinds of evil effects upon the drinker, could be had for a penny a tot, and the gaudy 'gin palaces' with their flaring lights were the only places where the poor man could buy an hour or two of noisy, cheerful company, and forget the miseries of the morrow.

The harsh contrast between the flaring gin palace and its pitiful surroundings inspired the pen of Charles Dickens in *Sketches by Boz*:

The gin-shops in and near Drury Lane, Holborn, St Giles's, Covent Garden, and Clare Market, are the handsomest in London. . . .

The filthy and miserable appearance of this part of London can hardly be imagined by those (and there are many such) who have not witnessed it. Wretched houses with broken windows patched with rags and paper: every room let out to a different family, and in many instances to two or even three—fruit and 'sweet-stuff' manufacturers in the cellars, barbers and red-herring vendors in the front parlours, cobblers in the back; a bird-fancier in the first floor, three families on the second, starvation in the attics, Irishmen in the passage, a 'musician' in the front kitchen, and a charwoman and five hungry children in the back one—filth everywhere—a gutter before the houses and a drain behind—clothes drying and slops emptying, from the windows; girls of fourteen or fifteen, with matted hair walking about barefoot, and in white greatcoats, almost their only covering; boys of all ages, in coats of all sizes and no coats at all; men and women, in every variety of scanty and dirty apparel, lounging, scolding, drinking, smoking, squabbling, fighting, and swearing.

You turn the corner. What a change! All is light and brilliancy. The hum of many voices issues from that splendid gin-shop which forms the commencement of the two streets opposite; and the gay building with the fantastically ornamented parapet, the illuminated clock, the plate-glass windows surrounded by stucco rosettes, and its profusion of gas-lights in richly gilt burners, is perfectly dazzling when contrasted with the darkness and dirt we have just left. The interior is even gayer than the exterior. A bar of French-polished mahogany, elegantly carved, extends the whole width of the place; and there are two side-aisles of great casks, painted green and gold, enclosed within a light brass rail, and bearing such inscriptions as "Old Tom, 549"; "Young Tom, 360"; "Samson, 1421"—the figures agreeing, we presume, with "gallons," understand. Beyond the bar is a lofty and spacious saloon, full of the same enticing vessels, with a gallery running round it, equally well furnished. On the counter, in addition to the usual spirit apparatus, are two or three little baskets of cakes and biscuits, which are carefully secured at the top with wickerwork, to prevent their contents being unlawfully abstracted. Behind it are two showily dressed damsels with large necklaces, dispensing the spirits and "compounds." They are assisted by the ostensible proprietor of the concern, a stout coarse fellow in a fur cap, put on very much on one side to give him a knowing air, and to display his sandy whiskers to the best advantage.

One of the outstanding features of London life at this time was the astonishing number of people who gained their living one way or another in the streets. There were newspaper-sellers, song-sheet sellers, dealers in second-hand goods, pedlars of all kinds of cheap drapery, sellers of every kind of food, both cooked and uncooked, the muffin-man, the cat's-meat man, and so on in endless variety. Something of this richness and variety of street-trading may still be seen in the open-air markets in different parts of London, but in the mid-nineteenth century the number and variety of these trades was far greater. There were, besides, all kinds of

A RABBIT-SELLER
After a print of 1805

street entertainers—showmen exhibiting freaks of all kinds, the flea-circus, the waxwork show, acrobats and sword-swallowers, strong men, performing monkeys, dancers and clowns, musicians and barrel-organs—the list is endless.

The costermongers of London formed a special class among the street traders with its own manners and customs, its own style of dress, even its own language, for the costermongers talked in a strange slang of their own which could not be understood by strangers. Indeed, when strangers were about they delighted in using this way of talking in order to mystify those outside their own circle. Many of the words from this costermongers' slang have found their way into the Cockney slang which still survives to some extent to-day.

Each costermonger either owned or hired a small cart pulled by a donkey, on which he hawked his wares about the streets, and on the whole they made a fair living, being very sharp and shrewd, and experienced in this kind of life, which was traditional with them. They looked down on the other street-traders, who were often people who had fallen out of employment. Such unfortunate people were usually unsuccessful and lived from hand to mouth, hardly making enough to keep themselves alive. The costermonger wore a kind of long waistcoat, with sleeves, made of corduroy, and with large bright buttons, often of mother-of-pearl. On his head was a small cap, and his corded trousers were tight as far as the knee and then swelled out over his boots. Even to-day some street-traders in London, descended from the old costermongers, possess these old costumes which they put on for special occasions such as horse-shows or the fair on Hampstead Heath on Bank Holidays.

Below the costermongers and the other street-traders in the social order of the London poor came a whole host of unlucky people who had no proper employment at all, and who scraped a living (if it could be called that) out of the dirt and refuse of the great city. In the business and better-class residential areas almost every street-crossing of importance had its crossing-sweeper, keeping the roadway clear of the mass of mud and horse-droppings which accumulated, and depending upon tips from the passer-by for his living. Often they were ragged bare-foot boys, but old men, old women, even girls, were to be found at this task. Still stranger occupations existed. There were the women who stood all day in the dust-contractor's yard, sifting dust and refuse for such articles as might be of value. There were the men who ventured into the old sewers at low tide, searching among the filth for scrap-metal, old bits of jewellery, coins, and other things of value swept down into the tunnels. There were the mudlarks, boys and old women mostly, who waded about in the mud left by the river at low tide, gathering up odd scraps of rope, pieces of coal, and other odds and ends of value dropped from ships. This was the underside of mid-Victorian London, the contrast to the solid comfort of Camden Town and Paddington or the aristocratic splendour of Piccadilly and Knightsbridge.

THE UNHEALTHY CONDITION OF MID-NINETEENTH-CENTURY LONDON

The unhappy condition of so much of the working-class population of London was, as we have pointed out, largely brought about by the speed with which London was growing. Until the middle of the century there was no authority with wide enough powers to look after the housing, the health, or the welfare of London's citizens as a whole. The problems arose before men had had time to work out a good way of governing London. There were other serious troubles besides slums and the lack of public help for the poor. For instance, the water-supply of London before 1852 was impure and insufficient. The New River, of which we wrote in an earlier chapter, was of course no longer able to supply the whole of London, though it still continued to be an important source of supply (as it still does). In 1721 the Chelsea Water Company was started, and in 1733 the Lambeth Water Company. By 1822 the Vauxhall Water Company, the West Middlesex, the East London, the Kent, the Grand Junction, and the Southwark Water companies had been added to the number. Sometimes competing companies were actually allowed to operate in areas which overlapped, so that two companies might be busy laying pipes in the same street at the same time, and touting for customers. Sometimes the workmen of rival companies actually fought in the streets.

More serious still was the fact that many of the companies took their water direct from the Thames as it passed through the central part of London, where it was polluted with all the filth allowed to flow into it. This water was pumped out to the customers without being filtered. The Lambeth water-works, for instance, obtained its water from the middle of the Thames at a point roughly where Waterloo Bridge now crosses the river. Even to-day we should hardly like the idea of drinking from the broad, greyish stream that flows under the bridge, but it is a great deal less polluted than it was in 1820 or 1840. Not only was the water-supply impure, but, bad as it was, it did not provide for every one. Thousands had no water-taps in their houses, and had to depend on public pumps. To make matters worse, there were districts where the company did not pump any water at all on Sundays. Thus many people were forced to use wells or even to take water from ditches. The wells were highly dangerous, for there were so many old cesspools and graveyards in London that the drainage from them poisoned the well-water.

The consequence of all this was that there were serious outbreaks of disease from time to time for which the water-supply was directly responsible. The most serious of these diseases carried by the water was cholera, which broke out several times between 1830 and 1855, carrying off thousands of people on each occasion. Ignorance and prejudice added to the difficulty of fighting this disease, as this extract from Charles Greville's diary shows:

Apr. 1, 1832. I have refrained for a long time from writing down anything about the cholera, because the subject is intolerably disgusting to me, and I have been bored past endurance by the perpetual questions of every fool about it. It is not, however, devoid of interest.

In the first place, what has happened here proves that "the people" of this enlightened, reading, thinking, reforming nation are not a whit less barbarous than the serfs in Russia, for precisely the same prejudices have been shown here that were found at St Petersburg and at Berlin. The disposition of the public was (and is) to believe that the whole thing was a humbug, and accordingly plenty of people were found to write in that sense, and the Press lent itself to propagate the same idea. The disease, however, kept creeping on, the Boards of Health which were everywhere established immediately became odious, and the vestries and parishes stoutly resisted all pecuniary demands for the purpose of carrying into effect the recommendations of the Central Board or the orders of the Privy Council. In this town the mob has taken the part of the anti-cholerites, and the most disgraceful scenes have occurred. The other day a Mr Pope, head of the hospital in Marylebone (Cholera Hospital), came to the Council Office to complain that a patient who was being removed with his own consent had been taken out of his chair by the mob and carried back, the chair broken, and the bearers and surgeon hardly escaping with their lives. Furious contests have taken place about the burials, it having been recommended that bodies should be burned directly after death, and the most violent prejudice opposing itself to this recommendation; in short, there is no end to the scenes of uproar, violence, and brutal ignorance that have gone on, and this on the part of the lower orders, for whose especial benefit all the precautions are taken, and for whose relief large sums have been raised and all the resources of charity called into activity in every part of the town.

Another great danger to the health of London arose from the lack of good drains. Many of the old sewers were in a ruinous condition and were partly blocked, giving rise to foul smells and an atmosphere dangerous to health. In any case, there was no general system of main drainage capable of dealing with the whole of London's sewage, and many houses, and even large blocks of buildings, still relied on huge cesspools. One reason for the slow progress in dealing with this problem was the lack of a central body with power to plan for the whole of London, but another reason was, probably, that the building of a big sewer-system is a very difficult affair, and for a long time there was not an engineer of sufficient knowledge and experience to tackle such a huge job.

All these social evils which beset the lives of the great majority of Londoners up to the middle of the nineteenth century—the uncertainty of employment, the poor wages, the bad housing conditions, the unhealthy state of water and sewerage, the lack of schools and of religious teaching—really sprang from two causes. The first was that Parliament was very slow to interfere with private trading, and therefore permitted bad employers to force down the level of wages. From about 1833, however, a series of Factory Acts were brought in to remedy the worst cases. Trade unions were also permitted after 1825, and began their long, slow struggle for better conditions. The activities of the Chartists also did much to improve the conditions of the working class and so did the activities of many private charities which sprang into existence once the need for them was realized. But these things are part of the general history of England, and can be merely mentioned in a book of this sort. Every manufacturing town in the country at this time was experiencing the same problems as London, though perhaps because of its greater size, London's problems seemed more pressing.

THE CONFUSED STATE OF LOCAL GOVERNMENT

The second reason, however, behind London's bad social conditions at this time is more directly concerned with the story of London's growth. This was the tangled state of Local Government in London. It may truly be said that until 1856 the public affairs of this huge area were in a state of chaos. A bewildering number of different bodies were concerned. There were the seventy-eight vestries, bodies rather like the local councils with restricted powers. Some of these had members regularly elected at proper intervals, others had members elected for life. Then certain other powers regarding bridges and main roads were exercised by the Justices of the Peace for Kent, Middlesex, and Surrey. The sewers were looked after by the Metropolitan Commissioners of Sewers. But, in addition, there was a host of different authorities with powers over lighting, paving, sewers, and construction of buildings. The number of these separate bodies amounted to the astonishing figure of three hundred. In many cases their authority overlapped, and none of them could be effectively controlled by the ratepayers. In consequence, there was, as we have seen, great inefficiency in the government of London, and there was also great waste, for such work as was done by these authorities was carried out only slowly, and at great cost.

It is not to be wondered at that these conditions existed. The growth of London had been so rapid that there had not been time to do more than to try to make old-fashioned institutions serve new needs. It was easier to build a great city than to think out good ways of governing it.

REFORM

But there were men in London who had begun to set about the long task of improving this ugly state of affairs. The searchlight of public inquiry was first directed to sanitary conditions. Edwin Chadwick, secretary of the Poor Law Commissioners, induced the Commissioners to order an inquiry into the sanitary conditions of London, in 1838. The report when presented to Parliament, in 1840, was so hideous that public feeling was aroused, and Parliament made a series of inquiries into conditions of life in London and other large towns. In 1847 and 1848 many useful Acts of Parliament were passed to improve the health, administration, and policing of large towns. In London the General Board of Health was set up, and began at once, in the face of much opposition, to attack the many evils in this field which cried out for remedy. But its work was hampered by the confusion which existed among the tangle of authorities which we have described above. In 1855 Sir Benjamin Hall, who was the President of the General Board of Health, introduced into Parliament a Bill designed to simplify and improve the government of London. It was called the Metropolis Management Bill. Under this Bill, which Parliament passed into law, real progress began to be made in improving social conditions. The Metropolitan Board of Works was set up, and between 1856 and 1888 it carried through a vast number of public improvements which changed the face of London and swept away many of the dark breeding-grounds of misery, crime, and disease.

THE BEGINNINGS OF BETTER THINGS

Foremost among the improvements undertaken by the Board of Works was the huge scheme for dealing with London's sewage. The work was designed and carried out by the Board's engineer, Sir Joseph Bazalgette, and was on a grand scale. The main part of the scheme was the construction of two main collecting, or intercepting, sewers, one on the north side of the Thames and one on the south. These main sewers were designed to collect all the flow from the local sewers and to carry it to two 'outfall' stations well down-river, where they could discharge into the Thames. The outfall stations were (and still are) at Barking, on the north side, and at Crossness, on the south. When this work was completed, in 1865, London had for the first time a complete system of sewage disposal, which ranked as one of the best in the world. London has since become one of the healthiest of the world's great cities.

This great work removed the biggest cause of pollution in the river. The second cause of river pollution, the great expanses of mud left exposed at low tides, was removed by the construction of a series of embankments, which also greatly improved the look of the riverside in the centre of London. The Victoria Embankment was opened in 1870, the Albert Embankment in 1869, the Chelsea Embankment in 1874. Many new streets were also cut through the maze of narrow side-streets and alleys which had grown up in some districts. Charing Cross Road, Shaftesbury Avenue, Northumberland Avenue, Hyde Park Corner, Queen Victoria Street, and Clerkenwell Road were a few of these new streets. Bridges were improved and rebuilt. Many of the bridges still charged tolls, and these were bought out. The Blackwall Tunnel was begun. A start was made with rehousing people in the worst of the slums. So year by year London changed more and more for the better under the influence of a central authority with power to plan and carry out large schemes of public improvements.

The Board of Works also took action which was much needed to save some open space for London. Already, of course, far too much open space had been built over without any thought being taken for such things as parks, open spaces, and recreation grounds. The London commons were in danger of being swallowed up in the steady spread of bricks and mortar. The Board of Works now joined in the fight with other public bodies and societies to save these commons, and also began to buy open spaces, or to contribute towards the cost of their purchase by the vestries and district boards.

THE LONDON COUNTY COUNCIL

However, for reasons which are now hard to understand, the Board of Works, which had done so much good for London, became at last unpopular and was accused of corruption. Finally, in 1889, London was made a county, with a county council directly elected by the ratepayers. Soon afterwards twenty-eight Metropolitan boroughs were created inside this new County of London to replace the multitude of vestries and district boards which had carried on its local government in such haphazard fashion. The ancient Corporation of the City of London retained the system of government which it had first worked out so many centuries before, and remained, in most of its functions, independent of the London County Council.

Henceforth Londoners had a clear system of local Government, and in 1889 the new council set about its great task with much energy and enthusiasm. Social conditions in London improved from year to year, and the London of the late nineteenth century was vastly different from the ill-governed, unhealthy metropolis of the forties and the fifties.

The boundaries of the County of London extended to Hampstead and Hackney, in the north; to Wandsworth, Lewisham, and Woolwich, in the south and east; and to Hammersmith, in the west. But the outward spread of London was not halted for a moment by the new system of government. It spread out farther and farther into Surrey and Kent, into Middlesex and Essex. A network of suburban railways provided fast transport in all directions within London, and served especially the large numbers of people who worked in the middle of London, but lived on its outskirts. Other means of transport also improved rapidly. The underground 'tube' trains began to run in 1890. Large numbers of horse-buses were also running by this time. So it became possible for more and more people to live in this great area called London, and to be able to get about quite easily from one district to another in the course of their daily business.

The great port became larger and larger, the docks spread farther and farther down-river—the St Katharine Dock, in 1828; the Royal Victoria, in 1855; the Millwall, in 1868; the Royal Albert, in 1880; Tilbury Docks (twenty-six miles from London), in 1890.

Fast Transport quickens London's Growth

Compared with the rate of advance between, say, 1815 and 1860, the growth of London in the last forty years of the nine-

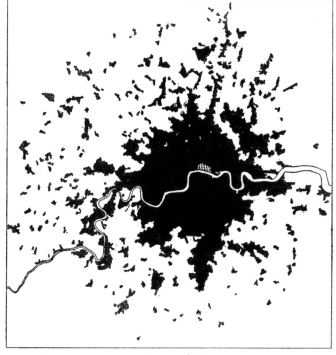

THE DISTRIBUTION OF LONDON'S POPULATION IN 1900

At the beginning of the present century London's built-up area continued to expand. The separate districts of South London had become one uninterrupted built-up area. Outlying suburbs and townships also were growing.

KEY

Black dots on white: Area of City of London.

teenth century was not quite so fast. But then, towards the close of the century, two fresh developments in transport helped enormously to increase the rate of London's growth. One was the use of electricity to drive trains. Not only were these put into service above ground, but it became possible from 1890 onward to start building the network of underground railways which is now so big that it seems almost like a separate world beneath the streets. The second and perhaps even more important invention was the internal-combustion engine. The first petrol-driven motor-bus ran from Victoria to Charing Cross in 1897. By 1905 the motor-bus was beginning to push the horse-bus off the streets. Before many years had passed the private motor-car and the taxi-cab were also playing their part in making it easier for the people of London to move about quickly and cheaply.

Thus it became easier than ever for people to live in the outlying suburbs of London and still be able to reach their work, even if it lay in the central districts or in some other district quite a distance from where they lived. Just as improved means of transport had had a powerful effect in aiding the expansion of the first half of the ninetenth century, so now in the first part of the twentieth century, up to 1939, improved transport was one of the chief causes of another spurt in London's growth.

The Population moves Outward

The population of the City and of the central districts showed a tendency to fall because people were going to live farther out. This movement was especially marked inside the boundaries of the old City itself, where London had first grown up. Already, in 1851, its population had fallen to 129,000. By 1911 this was down to 19,000, and by 1939 it had fallen to under 10,000. The population of the County of London area in 1901 was 4,540,000. It reached its peak in the next ten years, and then began to fall steadily but slowly. By 1938 it was 4,062,000, and by 1950 it was a good deal smaller still. But the population of Greater London as a whole continued to rise steadily to a total of about 8,500,000 by 1937. The map at page 132 shows the vast area covered by Greater London by 1945.

THE CITY'S FINANCIAL POWER

During this long period which we have been reviewing, stretching in all from about 1815 or 1820 to the eve of the Second World War, the City of London became the most powerful financial centre in the world. In recent times the damaging effect of two great wars and the growing strength of New York, the business capital of the United States, have affected London's position in this respect, but for long years the profits which Britain made by her leadership in the Industrial Revolution flowed into the City, where they were used for investment in all kinds of businesses in every country in the world. Besides dealing in money itself the City developed all kinds of special exchanges for dealing in grain, metals, furs, rubber, tea, and many other commodities. It was also the chief centre for insurance of all kinds, for the chartering of ships, and for many other kinds of business. All these activities, of course, still go on, and many have been rebuilt from nothing, after having ceased during the Second World War.

INDUSTRIES IN LONDON

Besides these activities of the City, and the great import and export business of her port, London became, during the nineteenth century and the first half of the twentieth, an important centre for all kinds of manufactured goods. Heavy engineering, chiefly connected with articles needed for ship repair, grew up near the docks, and light-engineering works of various kinds were found all over London. Other kinds of light industry, mostly supplying goods which can be easily sold in or round

I

London, have multiplied. Paint- and chemical-works, paper-
and printing-works, clothing and furniture factories, makers of
electrical goods, of boots and shoes—the list is endless. Even
motor-cars and tractors are made in London, if one includes the
Ford works at Dagenham. The production and sale of food,
drink, and tobacco also employs very large numbers of people.

The location of these factories varies widely; they are, indeed,
dotted all over London. But most of the chief industrial zones
lie outside the central area. Some are in Southwark and Bermondsey, others round the docks district in Rotherhithe, Millwall,
Greenwich, and Woolwich. An important belt of industry
stretches up the Lea Valley from the East India Docks, past
Stratford, to Upper Clapton and Lea Bridge. Other areas are in
Camden Town, Acton, and on the Great West Road. There
are also important industrial areas in the valleys of the Wandle
and Ravensbourne rivers, in South London.

ACTIVITIES OF "LONDON TRANSPORT"

Most of this development would not have been possible
without the free flow of goods and people made possible by
London's transport. The underground railways, in particular,
not only served the needs of existing parts of London, but by
extending lines overground into country districts on the outskirts encouraged the growth of the new suburbs. This sort of
activity continued when the underground railways and the leading bus and tramway companies were merged into the London
Passenger Transport Board, later replaced in turn by the London
Transport Executive. In this way the growth of the outer
suburbs such as Golders Green and Hampstead Garden Suburb,
at the beginning of the twentieth century, or of Hendon, Harrow,
and Edgware, in the twenties and thirties, was greatly speeded
up. Whole new towns grew round the railway stations which
at first had stood in small villages.

A Better Life for the Londoner of the Twentieth Century

It must not be forgotten that the steadily improving transport facilities also greatly increased the opportunities for the ordinary man to go in search of pleasure and recreation. The life of the ordinary man in London in the nineteen-thirties had indeed changed out of all recognition compared with that of his ancestors in the eighteen-sixties. His purchasing power enabled him to live decently, to clothe himself and his family properly, to buy enough food and fuel, to have a little over for books, radio-sets, and the like; cheap, comfortable transport took him to and from work, and enabled him to go to cinemas, theatres, and football matches, to visit friends, or to go out into the country. His children were educated at free schools; the local council and the county council, which he helped to elect, provided him with many public services designed to secure his health and safety and to improve his leisure. Though much remained to be done to improve social services still further, the improvement in the way of life of the ordinary man in the space of eighty years was immense.

From about 1890 onward much had also been done to improve the houses of the lower-paid people of London. Gradually the worst of the slums began to be cleared, and after the First World War this work was carried on with more vigour, for there was a strong feeling then that an improvement in living conditions was much overdue. As men returned from what had been, up to then, the worst war in history the phrase "a land fit for heroes to live in" was on every one's lips. From 1919 to 1938 £12,000,000 was spent in London on clearing condemned areas and rehousing the inhabitants. In addition a good proportion of the houses which were built during this time were of a type well within the means of those with quite modest incomes. Nevertheless, it still remained true that many thousands of the poorest people continued to live in drab, down-at-heel districts, where

THE DISTRIBUTION OF LONDON'S POPULATION IN 1945
By 1945 there had been enormous development of outlying
suburbs and townships owing to improved transport and migration
from Central London during the previous forty years.
KEY
Black dots on white: Area of City of London.

they were crowded together in flats or tenements often converted
from houses originally built to house one large family.

THE EXTENT OF GREATER LONDON

It is difficult to be precise about the limits which London had
reached by 1939. The mighty expanse of buildings and streets

had affected the growth, the trade, and the character of towns as far west as Maidenhead and Staines, as far east as Southend, as far south as Brighton, as far north as Watford, St Albans, and Hatfield. Various authorities had various areas mapped out which they regarded as London for their particular purpose. There is, for instance, the London Traffic area, which differs from the London Transport area. Both are different from the Metropolitan Police area, which again is different from the Metropolitan Water Board area. But, generally speaking, the area taken as Greater London is that of the Metropolitan Police District and the City of London. This vast area stretches from Barnet and Potters Bar, in the north, to Epsom and Coulsdon, in the south, from Uxbridge and Staines, in the west, to Romford and Dagenham, in the east. Its area is about 690 square miles and its population about 8,500,000.

To this has London grown, building and building endlessly round the tiny, independent City at its heart. All this has come about because the Thames is the gateway to England, because at one point on the banks of that great river two little hills and a bluff of hard ground overlooked the point where the tide ceased, where the river might be bridged, where road and river might meet, so that goods and men might come and go freely throughout the length and breadth of Britain, and, in the end, across all the oceans of the world.

Chapter Eight

TO-DAY AND TO-MORROW

Despite the rise of many other large cities in Great Britain in the last hundred and fifty years London has kept its leading position in the country. It is still, as it has been for so many centuries, the most powerful influence in every branch of the life of the nation. It includes about one-sixth of the total population of Great Britain, and controls perhaps a quarter of the nation's trade. It is the capital, not only of the United Kingdom of Great Britain and Northern Ireland, but also of the British Commonwealth and Empire. It is the centre of our financial and commercial life; every important business maintains offices in London, our chief banks have their head-offices there, and many of the most important business markets and exchanges of the world are held there. London is the chief centre of our system of communications by road, by rail, by air, by telegraph, and by radio. It is the centre of the artistic life of our country; all the most important theatres are there, the national art galleries and museums, the chief associations of artists, architects, and designers. It is the headquarters of fashion. The great book-publishing houses, the great newspapers, the broadcasting system, are all centred on London. Thus it has enormous influence, not only in Britain's trade, but on what is thought and said and written and created throughout the country and Commonwealth.

Every improvement in transport and communication has tended to increase this tendency for the life of the country to be centred on London. As we have shown, this has been a most powerful aid to its unending growth. By the nineteen-thirties it began to be generally thought that London was becoming far too big. Motor-cars and lorries had become very cheap, and the roads of the country were crowded with them. In London the traffic choked the streets, which had never been planned to carry such streams of vehicles. The problem of getting to and from work began to be a wearisome business for many people. Moreover, owing to the rapid growth of London in the past and the lack of laws to control it, there were huge districts in London with hardly any open spaces left, where factories and houses were jumbled together, and even the little back-yard which every Londoner likes to have behind his house was reduced to a few square yards.

As early as 1924 the London County Council began to plan large schemes for improving various parts of the County of London, and in 1927 the first Regional Committee for Greater London began to meet to see what could be done to safeguard London's open spaces and to control new building. In 1932 the passing into law of the Town and Country Planning Act made it possible for the London authorities to get more control over its growth. By 1935 the London County Council had planning powers for the whole of London County. The Greater London authorities saw the need for a 'green belt' of open country stretching round London to break the endless march of streets and houses out into the fields. In 1935 the London County Council offered to help with this idea by purchasing land up to a value of £2,000,000. Other authorities also took action, and a beginning was made in piecing together this belt of open country which could be saved from building.

In 1939 the Second World War broke out, and before long all the energy of London was turned to fighting back against the greatest attempt at destruction which it had had to meet since the Danish invasions of a thousand years before. In 1940 to 1941 and again in 1944 London suffered enormous damage; yet in the middle of this terrible struggle for survival thoughts were turned to the rebuilding and improvement of London after the War.

Two great plans were prepared, one for the County of London and one for Greater London. For the first time the problems of these great regions were surveyed as a whole and far-reaching plans suggested for their improvement.

After the War the most urgent need in London was to clear the bombed sites, to repair the thousands of houses damaged by bombing but still usable, and to begin building new houses, some permanent and some temporary, to replace those which had been destroyed. This great task has had to come before all other improvements, and not very much has been done to push on with the really big changes suggested in the new plans.

Every one knows the hard struggle that Britain has had to make in the last few years to recover from the effects of the War. Among other things, strict control of building of all kinds has had to be established, and in London this has meant that the outward spread of building has been practically stopped for the first time in hundreds of years. The creation of the new Ministry of Local Government and Planning (later the Ministry of Housing and Local Government), and the increased powers of local authorities, mean that all new building can be controlled in almost any desired way. The creation of the Land Development Board has also had a powerful effect in discouraging speculation in building-land. Thus it looks as if the green belt round London will indeed be preserved and a limit set to the size of Greater London.

This, however, can be made certain only if another part of the planning becomes fully effective. There are still many people in London without a house of their own to live in, many families living in flats or rooms too small for their needs. There is only a very little room left in Greater London in which to build more houses without interfering with the parks and open spaces. The only way to deal with this matter is to persuade large numbers of people, as well as the businesses and factories in which they work, to move right away from London. A start has been made with this. New towns are being built thirty or forty miles from

London which are intended to draw off some of the population and thus stop the urge for London to continue spreading. For this purpose certain small towns or large villages, such as Hemel Hempstead, Stevenage, and Crawley, have been chosen. They already have a life of their own, and round this nucleus the new areas will grow. It would be useless if these new satellite towns, as they are called, were to be simply places where people slept, going into London each day to work. That is why great care has been taken to ensure that industries as well as people move into the new towns. It will take a long time before really large numbers of people move out into these places, but the movement is beginning. It seems the only real hope of stopping the growth of London.

Something has also been done to begin refashioning the older districts of London in which overcrowding and the mixing-up of houses and factories is so obvious. In Poplar one complete district has already been rebuilt in this way, and this will fit into the general design of the County of London plan.

Every one knows that it is far easier to make plans than to carry them out, however worthy they may be. At the end of the War no one could foresee that the shortages of labour and materials in Britain would be as great as they turned out to be. It has not yet been possible to fix any definite periods for carrying out the various stages of the refashioning of London. But nothing stays still in a great city, and as alterations are made they can be aimed at gradually fulfilling the master plan. Its main points are: to relieve traffic congestion; to do away with overcrowding of houses, and to replace old, out-of-date houses; to provide more open spaces in districts where there are none, to sort out the tangle of dwelling-houses and industries which are mixed up together and often compressed into small areas between roads and railways. It aims also at defining the boundaries of Greater London, and at reducing the number of people in different areas.

This can be "the shape of things to come." Difficult it may be to make it come true, costly it certainly will be, but it is a purpose to which every Londoner should give his goodwill and such help as he can. It is a purpose infinitely worth while—to make this great and wonderful London a better place to live in. There are some who disagree with planning and control, but it is the lack of these things in the past which has made them more necessary now. But they must be wisely used. Nothing must be done to weaken London's links with the past, her many old and lovely buildings, the parts of old villages which still survive here and there like islands in a stream, in Highgate, in Chiswick, in Dulwich Village, in Shepherd's Market (in Mayfair), and in many other places. London is old and strong, and the secret of that strength is in the continuity of her history. London has grown, like a man or a tree, changing only that which must be changed, preferring always to adapt old places to new uses rather than to sweep them away. Merchants still do business in the City, where the Roman merchants first began; the lawyers are busy in the Inns of Court, where they settled in the Middle Ages; Billings-gate deals in fish, as it has done for centuries; the government of the country is still carried on in Westminster, as it has been for almost a thousand years. These are well-known things, but in every corner in London the inquirer will find that the link with the past is preserved somehow. In the public libraries are histories of each district; in clubs and societies lectures are being given by those who know and treasure the past history of even the newest suburb of London.

For two thousand years the advantages of the site of London have ensured the survival of a city at this point and have fostered its growth to almost unimaginable size. London is no single creation of a powerful prince, a gifted architect, or a hard-working committee. It is a living organism which owes its existence to certain great geographical and historical forces, working through the energy, the skill, the courage, the simple act of living of generations of men. It is a place of never-ending interest, and can be studied from a thousand different points of view. The meanest of its streets and the grandest of its monu-

ments are alike important to the student of London. If this book
has served to make the reader walk through the streets of London
with a more inquiring eye, if it makes him want to find out more
about the thousand separate stories which make up the story of
London's growth, it will have served its purpose.

BOOK LIST

BESANT, SIR WALTER: *London* (Chatto, 1892).

  A Survey of London (Black, 1909–12).

BOOTH, C.: *Life and Labour of the People in London* (Macmillan, 1902–3).

CHILDE, V. GORDON: *Prehistoric Communities of the British Isles* (Chambers, 1947).

COLLINGWOOD, R. G., AND MYRES, J. N. L.: *Roman Britain* (Oxford University Press, 1937).

DARBY, H. C.: *Historical Geography of England before 1800* (Cambridge University Press, 1936).

DEMANGEON, A.: *The British Isles* (Heinemann, 1939).

GIBBON, SIR G., AND BELL, R. W.: *History of the London County Council, 1889–1939* (Macmillan, 1939).

IVIMEY, ALAN: *A History of London* (Low, 1932).

MACKINDER, SIR HALFORD J.: *Britain and the British Seas* (Oxford University Press, 1902).

MAYHEW, HENRY: *London Labour and the London Poor* (Griffin, 1851).

ORMSBY, H. R.: *London on the Thames* (Sifton, Praed, 1924).

PEPYS, SAMUEL: *Diary* (1665–66).

QUENNELL, PETER: *Victorian Panorama* (Batsford, 1937).

RASMUSSEN, S. E.: *London: the Unique City* (Cape, 1937).

REDDAWAY, T. F.: *The Rebuilding of London after the Great Fire* (Cape, 1940).

SNOWDON, W. CRAWFORD: *London Two Hundred Years Ago* (Daily Mail, 1948).

STENTON, SIR FRANK M.: *Norman London*. A pamphlet of the Historical Association, with sketch-map by Marjorie Honeybourne (Bell, 1934).

STOW, JOHN: *Survey of London* (Oxford University Press, 1927).

TREVELYAN, G. M.: *English Social History* (Longmans, 1944).

  History of England (Longmans, 1926).

WINBOLT, S. E.: *Britain under the Romans* (Penguin, 1946).

Proceedings of the London Topographical Society.

ROYAL COMMISSION ON HISTORICAL MONUMENTS: *Roman London; the City.*

INDEX